Common Sense on Life Support

Roger Monarch Jr.

Published by MONARCH PUBLISHING, 2026.

COMMON SENSE ON LIFE SUPPORT

First edition. February 6, 2026.

Copyright © 2026 Roger Monarch Jr..

ISBN: 979-8994191408

Written by Roger Monarch Jr..

Table of Contents

How to Know If This Book Is Going to Hurt Your Feelings

I'm not a scholar. I'm not a historian. I'm not a professional talker with a podcast mic, a ring light, and hair product. Ask any of my old grammar school teachers and they'd tell you I was the last kid they thought would ever write a book. Back then, my biggest contribution to literature was doodling in the margins and trying not to get caught passing notes.

There were no publishers, no editors, no HR committee, and definitely no "allyship" involved in this project. So if you came here looking for a smart book, this ain't it. This book comes with no trigger warnings, no safe spaces, and zero apologies. There's no cry corner, no therapy puppy, and no adult coloring pages tucked in the back. It is not D.E.I.-certified, gluten free, or carbon neutral. If you need a hashtag to recover from a sentence, you're already in the wrong place.

If you think words are violence, silence is violence, and disagreement is a hate crime—close it now. Exit stage left. We keep participation trophies by the door. Grab one on your way out.

This one was written for grown ups.

If you've ever looked around and muttered, "What in the actual hell happened to common sense?"—pull up a chair. If you're tired of being told to celebrate nonsense, apologize for noticing reality, or whisper the truth because someone might get upset, you're home.

Fair warning: somewhere in these pages I'm going to offend you. That's a good thing. It means you're awake. And you need to be awake—not woke.

I'm not here to validate your feelings or hold your hand. I'm here to tell you what I've seen with my own eyes in a corner of Southeast Texas most of the country had never heard of until the T.P.C. explosion—the one that destroyed everyone's homes, the one where the company called bankruptcy and covered no damages. But that's a whole other book.

You don't have to agree with me. You don't have to like me. But if you can still shake a man's hand after you've argued with him, keep reading.

ROGER MONARCH JR.

I was born mid-'70s, raised through the '80s and '90s, when life had rules you didn't need a committee footnote to understand. You worked hard. You respected your elders. You stood up for yourself. And you accepted that not everybody was going to like you. It wasn't perfect—no time ever is—but it made sense.

Then the rules changed. And nobody asked if we wanted them to.

Now we've got schools asking four-year-olds to pick pronouns like they're choosing ice cream flavors. We've got corporations apologizing for things nobody found offensive five years ago. And we've got retirees in chicken and banana costumes calling it resistance. Question any of it, and suddenly you're the problem.

This book isn't about turning back the clock. You can't unring a bell, and I wouldn't want to anyway. Change happens. Some change is good. But I'm smart enough to know not all change is progress.

So here's the question nobody seems willing to ask anymore: Was the trade worth it?

Are our kids happier? Are our communities tighter? Is life better—or did we just swap one set of problems for a shinier, louder set and call it enlightenment?

What follows are the stories I've lived, the lessons I've learned the hard way, and the things I've watched unravel one thread at a time. Some will make you laugh. Some will make you mad. Some will make you nod so hard your neck hurts.

These stories are true, though I've changed the names to protect the innocent and the guilty. Southeast Texas is a small world. Some of y'all will recognize yourselves anyway. That's between you and Jesus.

I'm not saying my way is the only way. I don't care who you vote for, where you pray, or how you live. Just try to be decent. Shake hands when you're done arguing. And whatever you do—don't be an asshole.

If everyone followed that one simple rule, this book wouldn't need to exist.

Now turn the page. The circus has already moved into the neighborhood. The clowns are juggling, the ringmaster's shouting, and the elephants are stomping through your flowerbeds. Time to decide whether we're going to clap—or clean it up.

Chapter 1:

The Chicken Fried Steak
The Setup

I was sitting in a Beaumont diner, working through a chicken fried steak the size of a hubcap, when the chicken walked in. Not a joke, not a half-hearted Halloween attempt, but a full-body bright yellow suit, red comb bobbing, oversized orange feet squeaking across the floor. Right behind her came a banana, crowned with a Burger King tiara like she'd just lost a bet in the produce aisle royalty.

At first, I figured it was spillover from a costume party—it was close to Halloween. My grandkids used to sing that dumb "Chicken Banana" song that made four-year-olds laugh and made adults want earplugs. I smiled as they passed.

"My grandkids think you're a hit at their daycare," I said, trying to be nice.

The chicken froze like I'd yanked out a feather. The banana stiffened. Through the mesh eye holes, the chicken shot me a look like I'd insulted her entire species. The banana stared like I'd tried to peel her.

"We are NOT here for children," the chicken snapped.

"This is a protest," the banana added, dead serious.

"A protest," I repeated. "Against what?"

They exchanged a dramatic look, then shouted in perfect unison: "Kings."

I waited for a punchline. It never showed up.

"Kings? Like Burger King?" I asked. "Did McDonald's put you two up to this?"

"It's about Trump," the banana said, so fired up I thought the foam might start smoking.

That was my sign to exit the conversation. "Well, good luck with that," I said, turning back to my plate.

The chicken leaned down, beak right by my ear. "You will understand when you lose your freedom."

"The only thing I'm losing is my appetite," I muttered. Not sure if she heard me, but they both waddled out, squeaking like a rubber toy revolt.

The Parking Lot Parade

I paid up and stepped outside, ready to forget the poultry revolution. But weirdness has a way of doubling down. Up the street at Rogers Park, a small crowd waved signs. I thought maybe Girl Scouts were raising money. I pulled closer. These were not Girl Scouts. These were retirees dressed like Spirit Halloween threw up and nobody cleaned it.

A referee blew a whistle at nobody. A knight swung a plastic sword at the wind. Someone wore a pope hat like they'd lost a Vatican raffle. And every single one wore a Burger King crown.

Front and center stood that angry chicken again, sweating under the sun. The banana stood beside her looking like potassium-fueled rage. Their signs read:

NO KINGS

DEMOCRACY NOT DICTATORSHIP

RESIST

I sat in my truck, engine running, trying to decode the madness. Beaumont, Port Neches, Nederland—these places had always made sense. At least enough sense. But this? Adults in food costumes protesting "kings" in Southeast Texas?

I did what anyone does when the universe glitches. I Googled it.

Turns out it was a "national movement." Hashtags. Facebook groups. Dramatic posts warning about fascism and tyranny. They believed wearing a chicken suit and yelling at passing Nissans was saving democracy.

And it hit me: they had no idea what they were doing either. The costumes were the point. The outrage was the fuel. The logic was optional. They just knew they were supposed to be angry. So they dressed up and got angry.

Madness at Home

I watched a while longer. A few drivers honked. Most stared straight ahead like the strange might reach through their windows and drag them into it.

And right there in that parking lot, I realized something that had been creeping up on me for years: the crazy wasn't out there anymore. It wasn't just in New York or California, sealed inside cable news or trapped in the phone. It had come home.

I used to believe the madness lived on the coasts, in big cities, inside the TV. I thought if I turned off the noise, life would still make sense right here. So I did. Stayed off social media, didn't even watch the news. But that meeting in the diner made it clear—the screen wasn't the problem. It was just a window. The crazy I was trying to shut out was already standing in my own backyard, wearing a chicken suit and a Burger King crown.

Southeast Texas I knew

Growing up, our area wasn't a place for costumes and hashtags. It was oil, refineries, football, and Friday night lights. People argued, sure. They voted different, prayed different, lived different. But they didn't dress up like poultry to make a point. They didn't need costumes. They had words. They had grit. They had the ability to disagree without turning it into theater.

That's what struck me most about the chicken and banana brigade. It wasn't just silly—it was hollow. Performance without consequence. They weren't risking anything. They weren't solving anything. They were just playing dress-up in the name of outrage.

Real Protest vs. Pretend Protest

I remember real protests. Strikes at the plant when safety was on the line. Men standing outside the gates, not in costumes, but in work boots. They weren't yelling at passing cars for likes. They were fighting for their lives, their paychecks, their families. That was protest. It had weight. It had risk. It had consequence.

Compare that to a chicken suit in a park. One is survival. The other is spectacle. And spectacle doesn't change anything except how ridiculous we look to ourselves.

The Outrage Economy

What I saw that day was part of something bigger—the outrage economy. People don't know what they're mad about anymore. They just know they're supposed to be mad. So they dress up, shout slogans, and hope someone notices. Outrage becomes the product. Anger becomes the brand. Logic is optional.

The problem is that outrage without substance doesn't build anything. It doesn't fix bridges, feed families, or keep the lights on. It just burns energy. And eventually, it burns people out.

When outrage becomes theater, reality becomes optional. And when reality becomes optional, the collapse isn't far behind.

That chicken fried steak in Beaumont wasn't just a meal. It was the moment I realized the circus wasn't on TV anymore. It had moved into the neighborhood, squeaking across the floor in oversized orange feet.

Chapter 2:

The World That Still Made Sense
The Town That Raised Me

I grew up in Port Neches, Texas—hour east of Houston if traffic's kind, two hours if it isn't. Blink and you miss the sign..

Google will tell you we've got one of the biggest synthetic rubber plants on the planet and a chemical complex that could light half the state. Truth is, just about every dad I knew punched in "at the plant." The rest of us lived on the paycheck schedule they brought home.

It was tight. Not cozy tight—nosy tight.

You couldn't sneeze at the Market Basket without your mom getting a phone call before you hit the checkout line. If you acted a fool at school, the whole neighborhood knew the details before supper. It could choke you some days, but it was also a net. You fell; somebody caught you.

Most places don't have that anymore. They call it progress. I call it lonely.

The Rhythm We Lived By

Life had a beat you could set your watch to. Not lazy—just orderly. Nobody was trying to "hack" their day or post about "winning" at 6 a.m. You just lived it.

School kicked off at 7:45 sharp. You were in your seat or you were writing a note. Too many notes and the phone rang at home. The phone rang at home and your ass paid for it. No therapy session, no IEP for "not being a morning person." You figured it out.

When that last bell hit, we spilled outside and stayed there till the streetlights buzzed on. That was curfew, written by God and the electric company.

We rode bikes till the chains rattled loose. Played tackle football in the street with no pads and no tears. Built forts out of scrap lumber and imagination.

You didn't text "u up?" You pedaled your bike through the neighborhoods till you seen a pile of bikes in a yard. That's where your friends were and that was our GPS.

Supper at the Table

Supper was at the table. Whole family. No TV blaring in the background, no phones—mostly because we didn't have mobile phones yet.

You ate what mom cooked or you stared it down till it won. You said yes ma'am, no sir, please and thank you like your life depended on it—because some nights it felt like it did.

We talked. Out loud. With our mouths, sometimes full of okra and shame if we'd done something stupid that day.

That table wasn't just where we ate. It was where we learned. You heard about Dad's Day at the plant. You told Mom about the test you failed. Your brother got caught in a lie.

Nobody pulled out a phone to fact-check. Nobody live-tweeted dinner. You sat there, present, whether you wanted to be or not.

And you know what? That mattered. Because when the world sped up later, when phones arrived and everyone started eating in separate rooms staring at separate screens, something got lost.

Not just the food. The talking. The being known.

Homework at the Kitchen Table

Homework happened at the same table, right after the dishes were cleared. Mom might help with spelling. Dad might check your math, usually wrong but confident about it.

When the homework was finished, you packed your bag for tomorrow. Then, and only then, you were free. Maybe one more lap around the block on your bike. Maybe an episode of Dukes of Hazzard. Maybe just sitting on the porch listening to crickets.

Simple. Solid. It worked.

Nobody was optimizing. Nobody was "grinding." You just did what needed doing, and when it was done, you rested. The rhythm made sense because it had a beginning, a middle, and an end.

Now everything bleeds together. Work emails at dinner. Homework at midnight. Rest? That's for quitters.

We called it balance. Now we call it burnout.

Friday Night Religion

Ask anybody raised in PN-G country what Port Neches was famous for, and they'll laugh if you mention rubber or refineries. They'll say "Indians football" and look at you like you're slow

Friday nights at The Reservation—that's what we called the stadium—the whole town showed up. Band, drill team, cheerleaders, moms and dads, grandmas and grandpas.

If you were not in the stands, folks figured you were either dead or on house arrest.

It wasn't just a game. It was church. It was community. It was the place where the banker sat next to the welder, where the teacher sat next to the guy who fixed her car, where everyone—for three hours—was just part of something bigger than themselves.

You didn't have to like football. You went anyway. Because that's what you did.

Now kids have a dozen places to be on Friday nights, none of them requiring they show up in person. Streaming games from their bedroom doesn't build community. It builds isolation with a good Wi-Fi connection.

Saturday Morning Meant Work

Saturday morning you paid for your freedom. Mow the yard, wax the car, clean the garage, help Dad with whatever half-baked project he'd cooked up that week.

When he said "good enough," and not a minute before, you were cut loose.

Summer meant the city pool and a dollar's worth of quarters for the snow-cone stand. Rest of the year meant bikes, pickup baseball, or seeing how far you could ride before somebody's mom hollered for you.

There was no negotiating. No "But Dad, I have plans." Your plans started after his list was finished. That wasn't cruelty. That was teaching you the world doesn't owe you anything, and freedom is earned, not given.

Kids today grow up thinking everything should be instant. Food, entertainment, answers, success. Nobody taught them that good things take time and effort.

We learned that on Saturday mornings with a lawnmower and a list.

Sunday Was Non-Negotiable

Sunday was church clothes and Jesus till noon, then family and food till you couldn't move.

You could love it or hate it, but you went. Not because anyone checked your theology at the door—because that's what the family did together.

Church wasn't perfect. The sermons were long. The pews were hard. Some folks were hypocrites. But it gave the week bones. It created a rhythm: work, play, rest, worship, repeat.

Now Sundays look like every other day. No pause. No reset. Just more scrolling, more consuming, more of the same endless noise.

You don't have to be religious to see what we lost. We lost the idea that some time should be set apart. That some moments matter more than others. That rest isn't laziness—it's necessary.

We used to build our weeks around a day of rest. Now we're confused why everyone's exhausted.

The Mall Was Our Internet

Central Mall in Port Arthur was teenage headquarters. J.C. Penney, Sears,Chess Kingz, a food court with Corn Dog 7, a crusty arcade called Silver Ball, and a movie theater that smelled like popcorn and teenage panic.

Friday and Saturday nights, it was wall-to-wall kids doing laps like the Daytona 500 on foot. We weren't shopping—we were hunting. New haircut, new girlfriend, new drama. Who was holding hands by the fountain? Who just got dumped by the Radio Shack? New music at Ted's records

Giovanni's pizza for the regulars. Casa Olé for the fancy dates when you had ten whole dollars and a dream.

We learned how to talk to girls there. With actual words. Face to face. You walked up, heart hammering, and asked her to the movies.

She might say yes. She might laugh. She might ignore you completely. Either way, the whole mall saw it, and you lived. No screenshots. No viral humiliation. You dusted off your pride and tried again next weekend.

That's how you learned rejection doesn't kill you. Embarrassment fades. And courage is something you build, not something you're born with.

Now kids can't even order pizza on the phone without anxiety. They'll send forty texts before they'll knock on a door. We're raising a generation that can't look people in the eye because they never had to practice.

The mall taught us. Rejection by rejection, conversation by conversation, we learned how to be human with other humans.

The Drag

Soon as one of us got wheels, the universe got bigger. Nederland Avenue on weekend nights—wash the car, crank the stereo, pack six idiots in a five-seat Camaro, and loop the strip from Burger Chef to the Eckerd's parking lot and back.

Windows down, music loud, waving at every car like we were kings of the world.

Pointless. Perfect. Free.

We weren't going anywhere. That was the point. We were just being young, together, in public, with nothing to prove and nowhere better to be.

Now kids sit in their rooms, alone, doors closed, screens glowing. They're "socializing" through headsets and handles. They think they're connected because they're talking to people in twelve states.

But they're not learning how to read a room, how to crack a joke that lands, how to handle the silence when nobody knows what to say next.

The Drag taught us that. And we didn't even know we were learning.

The Last Days of Being Left Alone

We didn't know it, but we were living in the final years of real privacy. No smartphones, no Ring cameras on every porch, no permanent record of every dumb thing you ever said at fifteen.

You screwed up, you paid for it right then, and it died with the people who saw it. You could grow up, move three streets over, and be a whole new man. Nobody dug up the bones.

That world ran on rules nobody had to post on a billboard:

Streetlights meant go home

Raised voices at the dinner table got shut down quick

Teachers could still paddle you

Dads could still take the door off the hinges

Nobody called CPS—they called it learning the hard way.

It wasn't heaven. But damn, it made sense.

And when you grow up where consequences are quick and boundaries are real, you learn real fast what happens when they disappear.

Why It Worked

The world I grew up in wasn't perfect. People got hurt. Mistakes were made. Some folks had it harder than others, and not everything was fair.

But it worked because it had structure. You knew where you stood. You knew what was expected. You knew the rules weren't going to change based on how you felt that day.

That structure created freedom. Real freedom. Not the fake kind where you're "free" to do whatever you want and then collapse when life pushes back.

The freedom to fail and get back up. The freedom to be wrong and be forgiven. The freedom to grow up without a permanent record following you into adulthood.

We had room to be kids. To be stupid. To figure it out.

And that room—that space between consequence and catastrophe—is exactly what's missing now.

The Closing Beat

The world that made sense didn't fall apart in a day. It eroded slowly, one small change at a time. More cameras. More surveillance. More rules. More lawyers. More fear.

Parents got scared. Teachers got handcuffed. Neighbors stopped talking. Churches split. Families scattered.

And the rhythm that held it all together—the dinner tables, the Friday nights, the Saturday mornings, the Sunday rest—got drowned out by the noise of progress.

I'm not saying we should go back. You can't rewind the world. But I am saying we should remember. Remember what worked. Remember what mattered. Remember what we lost.

Because the next generation deserves to know there was a time when life made sense. When kids could be kids. When neighbors looked out for each other. When Friday nights brought the whole town together.

They deserve to know it's possible.

And maybe, just maybe, they can build something like it again.

Chapter 3:

Work, Consequences, and a Mouth Full of Ivory Chores Weren't Optional, They Were Oxygen

We didn't get "enrichment activities" or "personal growth opportunities." We got chores. A list on the fridge, and it better be done before Dad's truck pulled in the driveway.

The yard didn't mow itself. The dishes didn't walk to the sink. The trash sure as hell didn't take itself to the curb. You had responsibilities, and if they weren't done, your weekend disappeared before it started.

No participation trophies. No progress pictures for social media. No TikTok of you pushing a lawnmower for likes. You just did it.

Maybe you got five bucks if the grass looked like a golf course and the hedges didn't look like a drunk man attacked them with kitchen scissors. But the money was beside the point.

The point was learning that nothing in life shows up free. That effort equals reward. That if you want more than nothing, you move your ass.

Nobody explained this in a family meeting. You just knew. Because the consequences for not doing your chores weren't a lecture—they were immediate and unmistakable.

Soap:
The Original Cancel Culture

I dropped the F-bomb once in the house. Once.

I don't even remember why—probably trying to sound cool in front of my little brother, testing out some word I'd picked up at school. My mom came around the corner like a heat-seeking missile.

No lecture. No countdown. No "use your words" or "let's talk about appropriate language."

She just walked to the bathroom, came back with a bar of Ivory the size of a brick, and said, "Open."

She dragged that thing across my tongue like she was sanding a 2x4. It tasted like perfume mixed with regret and a chemical plant explosion. I gagged, drooled, cried a little. Nobody cared.

Then I had to rinse, look her in the eye, and apologize—with bubbles still coming out of my mouth.

You know what I learned? Words have weight. And some words cost you.

I never said that word in the house again.

Today, they'd probably call CPS. Back then, we called it learning. And it worked. Not because it was abuse   it wasn't. Because it was immediate, clear, and impossible to forget.

The punishment fit the crime, and then it was over. No files. No reports. No therapy sessions. Just a lesson learned and a nasty taste that lasted the rest of the day.

The Ventriloquist Pinch

If you acted up in public—threw a tantrum in Walmart, mouthed off at church, showed off in front of company—Mom couldn't exactly light you up in the cereal aisle.

So, she had another move: the Ventriloquist Pinch.

She'd keep smiling at whoever she was talking to, reach over, grab that tender strip of skin under your arm, and twist while whispering through clenched teeth: "Wait till we get home."

Her lips never moved. Her face never changed. She looked like a model parent having a pleasant conversation.

You, on the other hand, were fluent in pain.

That pinch was a promise. And if it didn't straighten you out right then and there, she had one final weapon—six words that struck more fear than any belt ever could:

"Wait till your father gets home."

That was death row with a five-hour appeal. You spent the whole afternoon imagining every possible outcome, replaying your crime, calculating your sentence. Half the punishment happened in your own head before Dad ever walked through the door.

By the time he got home, you were already broken. Sometimes he didn't even have to do anything. Just the look was enough.

That wasn't cruelty. That was psychological warfare at its finest. And it taught you something valuable: actions have consequences, even when nobody's watching. Especially when nobody's watching.

Doors Were Temporary Privileges

Talk back. Slam a door. Keep running your mouth after "no" already left somebody's lips.

You'd learn really quick that bedroom doors were removable.

Dad didn't need a YouTube tutorial. He didn't need power tools. Two screws, a hinge pin, or straight-up Hulk strength, and that door was leaning against the garage wall before supper got cold.

Try changing clothes with just a doorway and your little brother peeking around the corner laughing. You lose the attitude really quick.

Today they'd call it emotional abuse. They'd start a GoFundMe for your "trauma." They'd write think pieces about the psychological damage of losing privacy.

Back then? We called it consequences.

And you know what? It worked. Because the loss of that door wasn't the punishment—it was the reminder. The reminder that respect isn't optional, that your room is a privilege, and that the roof over your head comes with expectations.

You got the door back when you earned it back. Not before.

The New Way:
Rooms That Are Too Comfortable

Kids today have rooms that look like Best Buy showrooms. Flat screens. Gaming systems. Laptops. Tablets. Phones with unlimited data. Wi-Fi passwords memorized before they can tie their shoes.

You send them to their room as punishment, and they disappear into a digital paradise for six hours.

That's not discipline. That's a vacation.

Back in my day, getting sent to your room meant staring at four walls, maybe a radio if you were lucky, and a whole lot of time to think about what you'd done. Boredom was the punishment. And boredom made you reconsider your choices real fast.

Now? Kids would pay to be sent to their rooms. The punishment became the reward, and we wonder why nothing sticks.

If you want consequences to mean something, they have to cost something. Comfort isn't a consequence. It's a reward. And when you reward bad behavior with comfort, you get more bad behavior.

It's not complicated.

Fights, Blood, and Handshakes

Real bullying—the relentless, sadistic kind—is evil. Some kids got it worse than they should have, and I'm not pretending that didn't happen.

But not every shove was a hate crime. Not every bloody nose required a therapist. Not every conflict was trauma.

We had bullies. Not anonymous keyboard warriors hiding behind fake names. Flesh-and-blood kids with faces, fists, and reputations. They didn't send warning texts. They didn't care about your feelings or your pronouns. They pushed. They tested. They swung.

And you had to deal with it.

The Script of a Fight

If talking didn't work, you settled it after school.

The script was simple: meet behind the gym, a circle formed, some shoves, a couple of swings. Maybe a bloody nose. Maybe someone hit the dirt. Usually both of you were too tired to keep going after a minute.

Then it ended.

"You done?"

"Yeah, I'm done."

You shook hands. Or at least nodded. And then it was over. You went to class with a fat lip and a story nobody filmed. No viral video. No school board meeting. No permanent record. You bled, you learned, you moved on.

And here's the part nobody wants to hear: knowing you might actually have to back your mouth up with your hands made you think twice before running it. You didn't talk endless trash because the consequences were immediate and physical.

You learned to measure your words. You learned to walk away from fights that didn't matter. And when a fight did matter, you handled it, took your lumps, and got on with your life.

What We Lost When We Banned Consequences

Today, every conflict is a federal case. Fights don't end in handshakes—they end in suspensions, police reports, lawsuits, and therapy referrals.

We took away the outlet and wondered why the pressure kept building.

Boys aren't allowed to be physical anymore. They're told to "use their words," to "express their feelings," to "process their emotions." And when that doesn't work—because sometimes it doesn't—they're medicated, suspended, or labeled.

We're raising boys who've never thrown a punch, never taken a punch, never learned that getting hit isn't the end of the world. And then we're shocked when they can't handle conflict as adults.

The parking lot fights weren't pretty. They weren't smart. But they had an ending. And that ending taught lessons no classroom ever could:

You can survive being wrong

Pain is temporary

Respect is earned through action, not words

Most fights aren't worth having

Now we've got grown men who can't look each other in the eye, who send passive-aggressive emails instead of having hard conversations, who fall apart when someone disagrees with them.

That's not progress. That's regression wrapped in safety language.

The Closing Beat:
When Consequences Were Clear

Soap, pinches, missing doors, bloody noses—none of it was perfect. Some of it was harsh. Some of it crossed lines.

But here's what it taught us: the world has edges. Actions have costs. Respect isn't given; it's earned. And pain, whether physical or emotional, is part of growing up.

My parents weren't trying to be my friend. They weren't running a democracy. They were raising someone who could function in the real world—a world that doesn't care about your feelings, doesn't give trigger warnings, and doesn't pause the game when you need a break.

The consequences we faced were immediate, clear, and finite. You messed up, you paid the price, and then it was over. No permanent record. No lingering trauma. Just a lesson learned and a reason not to do it again.

Today's kids don't get that. They get endless second chances, participation trophies, and adults who apologize for setting boundaries. They grow up thinking consequences are negotiable, that rules are suggestions, and that discomfort is abuse.

Then they hit the real world—a boss who doesn't care about their anxiety, a landlord who won't accept excuses, a relationship that requires actual work—and they shatter.

We didn't do them any favors by padding every corner and removing every consequence. We just delayed the inevitable and made it hurt worse when it finally arrived.

Because here's the truth nobody wants to say out loud: when you take away real consequences, you don't get kinder, gentler kids.

You get adults who can't handle reality.

And reality doesn't negotiate.

Chapter 4:

The Reality War
Physics Does Not Negotiate

There's a divide in this country that cuts deeper than politics, deeper than red states and blue states, deeper than any election could ever fix.

It's the chasm between people who answer to physics and people who answer to feelings.

I spent years around plants, docks, and job sites in Southeast Texas. Out there, reality is the final boss. It does not negotiate. It does not care about your intentions. It does not grade on a curve.

If you're a welder and you lay a bad bead on a high-pressure line, that line can blow. If you're a rigger and you misjudge a load, a thousand-pound pipe swings into space and someone goes to the hospital—or worse.

Physics does not care if you're having a bad day. It does not care about your pronouns, your feelings, or your personal truth. If you're wrong, things break. People get hurt. People die.

There's no HR department for gravity. There's no committee meeting to discuss whether the bolt was torqued correctly. There's only the sound of something going terribly wrong and the desperate hope you're not standing too close when it does.

That world teaches a brutal and sacred kind of respect. It teaches you the limits of your own skill, the weight of your own mistakes, and the absolute necessity of getting it right the first time.

You don't get to lie to yourself out there, because the physical world calls your bluff in seconds.

The Birth of the Laptop Class

Then there's the other world.

People indoors, under soft lights and central air, wearing business casual and headsets. Their tools are email, PowerPoint, Slack, and Zoom. They move pixels on screens. They sit in meetings about "synergy" and "alignment" and "stakeholder engagement."

They call changing the color of a button on a website a "sprint."

This is the Laptop Class. Their work exists in the abstract. Their documents are weightless. Their tools fit in a backpack. Their mistakes don't draw blood.

I don't hate office people. Many work hard at difficult, complex tasks that require real intelligence and skill. But something fundamental changes when the cost of failure is cushioned.

When a welder messes up, someone might lose a hand.

When a marketing analyst messes up, someone schedules a follow-up meeting.

The worst thing that happens is another meeting, a stern email, or a performance review that goes in a file somewhere and gets forgotten by next quarter.

COMMON SENSE ON LIFE SUPPORT

When your mistakes are padded by HR policies and root-cause analyses, when failure means "let's regroup and try a different approach," it rewires your understanding of cause and effect.

You start to believe problems can be managed with the right language. That a memo can stop a fire. That reality is flexible, negotiable, a matter of perspective.

The Laptop Class lives by different laws. Not the laws of physics, but the laws of consensus, policy, and perceived truth.

The Consequence Gap

This is the heart of the divide: the Consequence Gap.

In the world of hands and steel, consequences are immediate, physical, and unforgiving. A mistake is a teacher that strikes fast. You learn, or you get removed from the equation—sometimes permanently.

In the world of laptops and video calls, consequences are delayed, social, and often negotiable. A mistake is a "learning opportunity." You explain, you reframe, you attend a training session, you update the documentation.

This gap creates two entirely different ways of seeing the world.

One group knows a pipe either holds pressure or it doesn't. A beam either bears the load or it buckles. The feedback is clear, immediate, and undeniable.

The other group knows a strategy is either approved or it isn't. A narrative is either compelling or it's boring. The feedback is ambiguous, political, and constantly shifting.

People in the real world correct their approach when it stops working. If your measurement is off, you buy a better tape measure and get it right.

People in the laptop world rewrite the rules instead. If your idea fails, you blame the rollout, the timing, the culture, the lack of buy-in.

One group gets hit by consequences.

The other gets hit by a calendar invite.

Where Fantasy Gets Manufactured

This is why almost every piece of modern cultural insanity gets manufactured in places far removed from physical risk.

Universities. Corporate HR departments. Government agencies. Nonprofits with mission statements longer than their budgets. Consulting firms that bill by the hour.

In these environments, you can spend months debating microaggressions in a departmental glossary because you're not worried about a crane collapsing. You can earn a degree studying theories that have no physical proof because nothing in your day requires proof.

You're not trying to get a diesel engine to turn over in the rain. You're not calculating the load on a foundation. You're not standing under a beam you just installed.

You can say things like "men can get pregnant" with a straight face because your daily reality never forces you to confront irreducible biology.

Biology isn't a daily, physical fact to you. It's a concept. A social construct. A topic for a panel discussion.

Try saying that same line to a framing crew on a hundred-degree day. They'll look at you like you've been sniffing paint thinner.

Not because they're hateful or ignorant. Because they deal with bodies, weight, exhaustion, and the sheer physical differential between a man and a woman when you're carrying eighty pounds of shingles up a ladder in July.

To them, biology isn't theory. It's the weight on their shoulder.

The Control of Language

Here's what happens next: when your ideas can't withstand contact with physical reality, you have to protect them from it.

You do this by controlling language—the very framework of discussion.

The people most disconnected from concrete consequences become the most obsessed with controlling speech and thought. They write the mandatory training modules. They draft the diversity statements. They roll out the new terminology across the company portal.

They're the ones who will never, ever look at a clearly absurd idea and say, "That's insane," even when everyone in the room is thinking it. To do so would violate the new rules of engagement, where feelings outrank facts and perceived harm trumps objective truth.

In the real world, you call a wrench a wrench. You call a leak a leak. The language is precise because the cost of confusion is high.

In the laptop world, language becomes soft, malleable, strategic. It's a tool for shaping perception, not for describing objective truth.

A firing becomes a "career transition."

A failure becomes a "learning opportunity."

A man becomes a "person with a prostate."

A mother becomes a "birthing person."

Late becomes "schedule-challenged."

This isn't evolution. It's evasion.

By controlling the words, the Laptop Class seeks to build a protective bubble around their ideas—a bubble that physical reality cannot pop.

The Two Americas

We're not just in a culture war. We're in a Reality War.

Two Americas are forming, speaking different languages, living by different rules, and answering to different gods.

One America wakes before dawn. Their hands are cracked, their boots are scuffed, they smell like diesel and sweat by lunchtime. They make things, fix things, grow things, and move things.

They live in a world of tangibles, where your word is your bond because the community is small and your reputation is everything. They understand that not all problems have solutions, but all solutions require work.

They know the difference between a good day and a bad day isn't how you feel about it—it's whether the job got done.

The other America logs on after coffee. Their hands are smooth, their offices are climate-controlled, their biggest physical exertion is carrying a laptop bag. They manage things, optimize things, and comment on things.

They live in a world of narratives, where perception is reality and the right words can change anything. They believe every problem has a policy solution, that progress is inevitable, and that anyone who disagrees just needs more education.

One group sees a world of hard limits and sharp edges.

The other sees a world of infinite malleability where everything is up for debate.

These two Americas are increasingly alien to one another. They don't just disagree on taxes or healthcare. They disagree on the fundamental nature of reality itself.

The Bill Is Coming

Fantasy can win for a while. But eventually, the bill comes due.

The Laptop Class has been running up a tab for years, building a society on feelings and abstractions while depending entirely on the physical world they disrespect and ignore.

The power for their laptops? Comes from plants run by people who understand thermodynamics.

The steel in their buildings? Forged by people who know metallurgy.

The food in their refrigerators? Grown, picked, packed, and delivered by people who work with dirt and sweat and diesel.

This can't last forever. Reality always collects.

You're seeing the early invoices now:

Supply chains breaking down because nobody wants to drive trucks anymore

The power grid straining because infrastructure was neglected for green fantasies that don't scale

Skilled trades aging out with no one to replace them because a generation was told real work was beneath them

Cities crumbling because the people who know how to fix them can't afford to live there

The reckoning won't arrive as an argument won in a conference room.

It'll arrive as a collapse. A blackout. A bridge closure. A shortage. A breakdown so obvious even the laptop can't spin it away.

The concrete world will reassert its primacy in the most concrete ways possible.

What Happens When the Lights Go Out

Picture this: it's summer in Texas. Temperature hits 105. The power grid fails—not for an hour, but for days.

The Laptop Class sits in their homes, laptops dead, AC off, scrolling their phones until the batteries die. Then they wait. And complain. And post about it until they can't anymore.

The Real-World Class? They've already pulled out generators, checked on elderly neighbors, fired up grills to cook the food before it spoils, rigged fans to battery packs, and organized work crews to help whoever needs it most.

They don't debate the politics of infrastructure. They deal with the reality of no power.

The Real World doesn't need to win the debate. It just needs to wait.

Because while the Laptop Class is drafting the disaster response plan, reality will be the disaster. And it won't care about the plan.

A Call for Grounding

This isn't a call to abandon thought, progress, or innovation. It's a call for grounding.

We need to tether our ideas back to the physical world. We need to respect the people who live there. We need to measure our grand philosophies against the unyielding ruler of reality.

If your brilliant idea can't explain how to keep the lights on, how to build a house, or how to feed a city, it's not a philosophy for humanity. It's a parlor game for the privileged.

The healing of this divide begins with a simple, humbling acknowledgment:

We are all physical creatures in a physical world. Our survival depends on those who understand that world most intimately.

The welder, the farmer, the lineman, the mechanic—they're not relics of a bygone era. They're the foundation. Before a single word of any policy document gets written, their work must be done.

The future doesn't belong to those who craft the most compelling fantasy. It belongs to those who can build, repair, and innovate within the stubborn, beautiful, non-negotiable limits of the real world.

The Closing Beat

The Reality War will end not with one side conquering the other, but with a rediscovery of common truth:

We all, ultimately, answer to physics.

And physics does not care about our feelings, our policies, our narratives, or our best intentions.

It only responds to our respect.

The Laptop Class can keep building castles in the clouds. But when the storm comes—and it will—those castles will vanish like they were never there.

The structures built by hands, steel, and sweat?

Those will still be standing.

Chapter 5:

The First Cracks
The Detention Slip

The first crack in the system showed up in a middle school hallway. One of the boys came home with a detention slip for fighting. He was in seventh or eighth grade, late '90s or early 2000s. He stood there in the kitchen, shoulders down, toes grinding the floor.

"I didn't start it," he said. "This kid's been shoving me, calling me names for weeks. I finally hit him back like you told me."

That was exactly what I had taught him. You don't start trouble, but you finish it if someone won't leave you alone.

"Don't worry," I told him. "Principal's an old coach of mine. We'll get this straight tomorrow."

I should have known better.

Hands Tied

The next morning, I walked into the same school I'd gone to as a kid. Same brick walls. Same scuffed floors that always smelled like wax and sweat. The man behind the desk—we will call him Coach Henderson. Coach Henderson—had paddled me more than once back in the day. We still laughed about that when we ran into each other at the store.

I figured this would be two old-timers talking sense.

I slid the slip across his desk. "Coach, he's been pushed around for weeks. He stood up for himself. Can we make this go away?"

He leaned back and let out a long breath. It wasn't the coach I remembered. It was a man boxed in.

"Can't do it," he said.

I laughed because I thought he was joking. "You paddled me for less than this."

"I did," he said. "But it's not up to me anymore."

That's when he said it:

"Zero tolerance. Both kids get the same punishment. District policy."

"You're the principal," I said. "You know what actually happened."

He lifted his hands. "Doesn't matter. My hands are tied."

And just like that, judgment was gone. Context didn't matter. Right and wrong didn't matter. The only thing that mattered was the policy.

How We Got Here

By the '90s, schools had been sued over everything. Some cases were real problems. Others were parents who couldn't accept that their kid wasn't perfect.

Instead of dealing with the troublemakers and the bad calls, districts did what big systems love to do: they wrote rules that replaced human judgment.

Flowchart justice.

Fight? Suspend everyone.

Butter knife in a lunchbox? Zero tolerance, maybe call the cops.

A burst of anger? Bring in the "threat team."

It looked neat in a binder. It sounded "fair" in a meeting. Nobody could accuse you of favoritism if you treated every situation like the same situation.

But in real life, it was chaos dressed as order.

Principals became rule readers instead of leaders.

Bullies and victims got punished together.

Schools became safer for lawsuits than for kids.

The Lesson

He served the detention. Later, he asked, "Why am I getting punished for doing the right thing?"

I could have dodged it. I could have said, "That's how life works." But that felt like feeding him a lie.

So, I told him the truth:

"Sometimes doing the right thing costs you. But that kid knows you're not prey anymore. That matters."

The bully never touched him again.

The slip didn't stop bullying. The punch did.

The Domino Effect

That detention slip was the first domino for me. The first time I saw the shift we're living with now.

"I agree with you, but my hands are tied."

"It's out of my control."

"Policy says..."

Schools. HR. Corporate rules. Speech codes. Social media bans. Sports regulations.

Judgment replaced by compliance.

Common sense replaced by fear.

If Coach had been allowed to be the man he used to be, it would have gone like this:

Bullying kid: three-day suspension. Hands off people.

My kid: free to go. Stand up for yourself. Next time, tell me sooner.

That would have taught everyone something real.

Actions have consequences.

Victims are not punished.

Adults are watching and willing to act.

The Human Cost

Instead, we taught kids that fairness means identical punishment no matter who did what.

We taught them that authority can't be trusted to think.

We taught them that it's safer to keep your head down than to defend yourself.

Then those kids grew up. And now we wonder why so many freeze when life gets rough, expect someone else to fix their problems, or report every disagreement like it's a crime.

The world is still full of bullies. It always will be.

No policy is going to change that.

What changes the world is kids who learn early that right is worth the price.

Do the right thing anyway.

Because the cost of silence is much worse.

Cultural Critique

Zero tolerance didn't just change schools. It changed culture. It taught kids that context doesn't matter. That judgment is dangerous. That rules are safer than thinking. And once you teach that lesson, it spreads. Into workplaces. Into politics. Into families.

We built a world where people say, "I know it's wrong, but my hands are tied."

We built a world where people punish everyone to avoid punishing the guilty.

We built a world where common sense is replaced by compliance.

And once that crack appears, the whole wall starts to crumble.

Closing Beat

That detention slip wasn't just about a fight in a hallway. It was about the first crack in a system that used to make sense.

And when judgment disappears, justice disappears with it. And when justice disappears, the cracks don't stop—they spread.

Chapter 6:

What Saved Me Would Be Banned Today
The Walkman Lifeline

I'm not exaggerating when I say music kept me alive. My teenage years in Port Neches had all the structure and common sense I've already laid out—streetlights for curfew, soap for punishment, football for belonging. But inside, I was a mess. Angry. Depressed. Restless. I didn't have words for any of it, and I sure as hell didn't trust anyone enough to talk about it.

We didn't have "mental health awareness months." We had "walk it off" and "you'll be fine." Some kids were fine. I wasn't. But I had a cheap Walkman, a stack of cassettes, and five voices that spoke when I couldn't: Robert Smith of The Cure, Trent Reznor of Nine Inch Nails, Marilyn Manson, Maynard James Keenan of Tool, and later on Corey Taylor of Slipknot.

They didn't hand out affirmations. They didn't tell me I was special. They screamed, whispered, and bled the same confusion and rage I was carrying around. Today, half of what saved me would probably be labeled "harmful," "problematic," or "too dark for young minds." That's the tragedy. The very art that kept some of us here is now treated like a threat.

The Cure:
Sadness With a Soundtrack

It started with The Cure. My cousin left a cassette of Kiss Me, Kiss Me, Kiss Me at our house. One night when I couldn't sleep, I slipped it into my Walkman. "Just Like Heaven" hit first—perfect pop. But it was the darker songs that got under my skin. "The Kiss." "A Forest." "Lullaby."

Robert Smith's voice sounded like somebody had crawled inside my chest and put my fog into words. He didn't sing about dramatic movie-style tragedy. He sang about that nameless heaviness, the feeling of being out of sync with the world for no clear reason, the ache you can't explain without sounding crazy or ungrateful.

Therapists today might say, "Don't listen to that, it feeds your depression. You need uplifting music." Here's what they miss: The Cure didn't make me sad. I was already sad. The music told me I wasn't the only one. There's a huge difference between art that glorifies misery and art that honestly describes it. One drags you down. The other keeps you company while you climb out.

Nine Inch Nails and Manson:
Doubt and Rage

Then came Trent Reznor. Pretty Hate Machine. One late night, the video for "Head Like a Hole" played on MTV for the first time. I had no idea what I was watching, but I was hooked. I bought the album. I wasn't ready for it, but I needed it anyway.

He didn't tiptoe around big questions. He screamed them straight to God.

Why am I in pain?

Why does God feel silent?

Why does everything feel fake?

Are you even really there?

Songs like "Ringfinger," "Sanctified," and especially "Terrible Lie" didn't give easy answers. They didn't wrap doubt in a church-approved sermon. They stood in the middle of the storm and refused to pretend.

Church folks called it blasphemy. They warned kids like me that this music would drag us straight to hell. They had it backwards. Reznor wasn't recruiting for Satan. He was telling the truth about what it feels like when God doesn't seem to answer. That honesty kept a lot of kids alive who might've given up if they felt completely alone with those thoughts.

And when sadness and doubt curdled into pure anger, Marilyn Manson showed up. Antichrist Superstar. Mechanical Animals. Holy Wood. Songs like "The Beautiful People," "Coma White," and "The Reflecting God." Manson confirmed what I'd already begun to suspect: authority is often a joke, religion is often a hustle, and the world is often more interested in control than truth. The best part is he said it with two middle fingers up and no apologies.

Then came Columbine in April 1999. Two teenagers murdered their classmates. The country needed a villain. They decided it was Manson. Never mind the shooters didn't like his music. Never mind there was no evidence his records had anything to do with the attack. None of that mattered. He was weird, offensive, and easy to hate.

Politicians held hearings. Parents burned CDs. Pundits preached that "this kind of music" was corrupting youth.

Meanwhile, kids like me were in our rooms, screaming those lyrics into pillows instead of at people. Getting it out of our systems. They blamed the vent, not the pressure.

Tool and Slipknot:
Pain Without Pamphlets

Maynard James Keenan and Tool were different. You couldn't always understand the lyrics on the first listen. Sometimes not even on the tenth. But you felt the weight. Albums like Ænima and Lateralus weren't about "feeling better." They were about seeing deeper.

Maynard went after stupidity, corruption, hypocrisy, and our own self-destructive habits. He didn't give slogans. He gave puzzles that forced you to sit with hard questions and think. Religious groups called it occult, demonic, and dangerous. But the real threat Tool posed wasn't spiritual. It was intellectual. He pushed kids to think for themselves, to question, to doubt, to take apart the stories they'd been given and look underneath. That kind of curiosity scares any institution built on obedience.

And then there was Slipknot and Corey Taylor. By the time I found them, I was older. More bitter. Done pretending. Songs like "People = Shit," "Spit It Out," and "Left Behind" weren't sophisticated philosophical statements. They were a pressure valve. I'd crank those records until the walls rattled and scream along until my lungs hurt. By the time the album ended, so did the worst of the anger. I could breathe again.

Did that music create violence? For me, and for a lot of kids like me, it prevented it.

The Scapegoat Cycle

There's a script society runs every time something terrible happens. A tragedy hits. People are scared and hurting. Instead of facing the real, complicated causes, leaders look for something simple to blame. They land on art, music, movies, games, and comedians.

They demand bans, labels, and censorship.

We saw it in the '80s with the PMRC. Tipper Gore and company dragged musicians like Dee Snider into hearings. Parental advisory stickers. "Satanic panic." Record burnings.

We saw it with Judas Priest in 1990, sued because two fans tried to kill themselves and someone claimed there were "subliminal messages" on a record.

We saw it with Manson after Columbine. We see it now when comedians get deplatformed, old sitcom episodes disappear from streaming, or artists are forced to apologize for lyrics written twenty years ago.

The story's always the same: instead of admitting the culture is sick, families are broken, kids are isolated, schools are failing, mental health is crumbling, we blame the mirror.

Smash the record. Delete the special. Pull the movie. Problem solved.

Except it isn't.

What Dangerous Art Really Does

Looking back, here's what those five artists did for me and still do.

Robert Smith witnessed sadness.

Trent Reznor witnessed doubt.

Marilyn Manson witnessed rage.

Maynard James Keenan witnessed confusion.

Corey Taylor witnessed exhaustion.

They didn't hand me a list of correct beliefs. They didn't give me a therapy worksheet. They gave me permission to feel what I actually felt. That permission kept me from exploding.

These days, people say, "That's too dark. Kids shouldn't listen to that. It might make them worse." They've got it backwards. The darkness was already there. The music was the flashlight.

If you want to "protect" kids by banning everything that makes you uncomfortable, you won't make their pain disappear. You'll just make them feel alone with it. Art that offends is usually art that tells the truth about something we don't want to face.

Silence that art, and you don't make the truth go away. You just blindfold the people who need to see it most.

A Message to Parents

If your kid is locked in their room blasting something that sounds dark or angry, don't start by ripping off the headphones.

Start by asking:

What is this song saying that hits you?

What is it about this band that you connect with?

What's going on in your world right now?

The music isn't making them feel that way. It's showing you that they already do.

You don't have to love the sound. You don't have to agree with the lyrics. But you'd better respect the signal. Because that might be the only place your kid is telling the truth out loud.

Closing Beat

I'm here with scars, kids, and grandkids because some artists refused to sanitize pain. They offended people. They scared churches. They outraged parents. And they kept people like me alive. They still do.

They called it dangerous

Chapter 7:

Comedy, TV, and Movies
When Jokes Had Teeth
The Midnight Realization

It was 2 a.m., and I was flipping through channels, trying to find something to knock me out. I landed on an old George Carlin special—You Are All Diseased, I think. Five minutes in, I sat up in bed. Not because I was laughing, but because I realized: This would never fly today.

Not because it wasn't funny. Because it was too honest.

Carlin was ripping into everything—religion, politics, corporate greed, our own hypocrisy. He wasn't just telling jokes. He was holding up a mirror to the absurdity of the world and daring you to look. And the audience was eating it up, not because they agreed with every word, but because they recognized the truth in it.

Now? If a comedian even hinted at half the things Carlin said, they'd be canceled before the punchline landed. The mob would descend, the clips would go viral, and the next thing you know, the comedian's career would be over—not because they weren't funny, but because they refused to tiptoe around the truth.

That's when it hit me: We've lost the ability to laugh at ourselves.

Stand-Up:
When Comedians Were Truth-Tellers
George Carlin:
The Man Who Said What We Were All Thinking

George Carlin didn't just tell jokes. He dissected the world with a surgeon's precision and a stand-up comedian's timing. His bit on the "Seven Words You Can Never Say on Television" wasn't just about swearing—it was about who gets to decide what we can and can't say. He didn't just push boundaries; he exposed how arbitrary they were.

I remember watching him on TV as a kid, sneaking glances when my parents weren't looking. Carlin didn't care if you were offended. He cared if you were paying attention. And that's what made him dangerous—not to society, but to the people who wanted to control it.

Richard Pryor:
Laughter as a Weapon

Richard Pryor didn't just make you laugh. He made you feel. He took the ugliest parts of life—racism, addiction, poverty—and turned them into something so raw and real that you couldn't look away. His use of the N-word wasn't about shock value. It was about reclaiming a word that had been used to dehumanize him and exposing the absurdity of its power.

I'll never forget the first time I heard his Live on the Sunset Strip album. Pryor talked about setting himself on fire while freebasing cocaine. It wasn't funny. It was terrifying and hilarious at the same time, because he was laughing at the pain, not glorifying it. That's what real comedy does—it takes the things we're afraid to talk about and forces us to confront them.

Eddie Murphy:
The King of No Sacred Cows

Eddie Murphy's Delirious was a masterclass in equal-opportunity offense. He roasted everyone—Black, white, gay, straight, men, women—and the audience loved it because it was real. Murphy didn't care about your feelings. He cared about the joke. And in doing so, he exposed the ridiculousness of the divisions we create.

I saw Delirious for the first time at a friend's house. We were maybe 14, and we thought we were the coolest kids alive because we were watching something so "adult." But what stuck with me wasn't the shock value. It was the freedom of it. Murphy wasn't performing for approval. He was performing for truth.

The Death of Dangerous Comedy

Now? Comedians are told what they can and can't say. They're given lists of "off-limits" topics and warned about "punching down." The result isn't cleaner comedy. It's blander, safer, and far less interesting.

Dave Chappelle got canceled for joking about transgender issues. Ricky Gervais gets death threats for mocking Hollywood's hypocrisy. Even Jerry Seinfeld—the king of observational, inoffensive humor—says he won't perform at colleges anymore because students are too "PC."

What's left is a generation of comedians who are more worried about not offending anyone than they are about being funny. And that's not comedy. That's a hostage situation.

Sitcoms and Movies:
When TV Had Balls
All in the Family:
The Bigot We Loved to Hate

All in the Family was revolutionary because it didn't just show you a bigot—it showed you why he was a bigot. Archie Bunker wasn't a hero. He was a flawed, stubborn, often infuriating man. But the show didn't let you off the hook by just laughing at him. It forced you to see the humanity in him, even when he was dead wrong.

That's what's missing today. We don't get characters who are allowed to be complicated. Now, every character has to be a hero or a villain, with no room for the messy, contradictory reality of being human.

Married... with Children:
The Anti-Sitcom

Married... with Children was the antithesis of everything TV was supposed to be. Al Bundy was a miserable, lazy, often cruel man. Peg was a ditzy, materialistic housewife. Their kids were selfish and dumb. And yet, the show was hilarious because it was honest.

It didn't preach. It didn't moralize. It just showed you a family that was as dysfunctional as most real families and let you laugh at the absurdity of it all.

Today? A show like Married... with Children would never get made. Al Bundy would be labeled a "toxic male." Peg would be called a "bad feminist." The kids would be diagnosed with ADHD and put on medication.

Blazing Saddles
and
Tropic Thunder:
Satire That Cut Deep

Blazing Saddles and Tropic Thunder are two of the greatest satirical films ever made because they used offense as a weapon. Mel Brooks didn't just mock racism in Blazing Saddles—he exposed how ridiculous it was by pushing it to its most absurd extremes. Robert Downey Jr.'s performance in Tropic Thunder wasn't just shocking—it was a brutal commentary on Hollywood's hypocrisy.

Both films would be impossible to make today. Not because they weren't brilliant, but because we've lost the ability to understand satire. Now, if a movie offends someone, it's not a sign that it's doing its job. It's a sign that it needs to be banned, edited, or "recontextualized."

What We Lose When
We Ban Offense

When we strip comedy and storytelling of anything that could offend, we don't just lose jokes. We lose the ability to confront uncomfortable truths.

Comedy used to be a release valve for the pressures of life. It let us laugh at the things that scared us, angered us, or confused us. It gave us a way to process pain without having to face it head-on.

Now, we've turned comedy into a minefield. Every joke is scrutinized. Every punchline is dissected for potential offense. And the result isn't a kinder, more inclusive world. It's a world where nobody dares to say what they really think.

The Cost of "Safe" Comedy

"Safe" comedy doesn't challenge anything. It doesn't make you think. It doesn't make you feel. It just fills time.

And that's not just bad for comedy. It's bad for us.

Because when we lose the ability to laugh at ourselves, we lose the ability to see ourselves clearly. We become so fragile that we can't handle a single joke at our expense. And that's not strength. That's weakness disguised as virtue.

A Word to the Perpetually Offended

If a joke stings, if a scene makes you uncomfortable, if a song pisses you off, ask yourself this: Why is this hitting me so hard?

Sometimes, it's because the artist is just being an ass. That happens.

But a lot of the time, it's because they've bumped up against a truth you've been avoiding.

Richard Pryor didn't make racism okay. He made it impossible to ignore. Mel Brooks didn't make bigotry noble. He made it look as stupid as it is. Eddie Murphy didn't make sexism acceptable. He made it so absurd that you couldn't take it seriously.

That's what great comedy does. It shines a light on the things we'd rather keep in the dark. And if you turn off that light, those things don't disappear. They just get harder to see.

So, before you demand that a joke be erased, a movie be banned, or a comedian be canceled, ask yourself: Am I offended because this is wrong, or because it's true?

The Pattern Repeats

From music to comedy to movies, the pattern is the same:

Artists push boundaries. They say the things we're all thinking but are too afraid to voice.

The outrage mob descends. They clip the most offensive parts out of context and demand the artist be silenced.

The artist is canceled. Their work is scrubbed from platforms, their career is ruined, and the world becomes a little less honest.

We pretend this makes us better. But all it does is make us more fragile, more divided, and more afraid of the truth.

The problem isn't that our art has gotten too dark or too offensive. The problem is that our lives have gotten too sanitized, and we've forgotten how to handle the messiness of being human.

Just Want to Say Thanks

To the comedians who refuse to bow to the outrage mob:

- **Dave Chappelle**—for telling the truth even when it costs him.
- **Ricky Gervais**—for mocking the powerful and never apologizing.
- **Bill Burr**—for saying the things we're all thinking but won't admit.
- **Joe Rogan**—for giving a platform to voices that get silenced everywhere else. **Bill Maher**—for being the last man on TV who still believes in free speech. **Matt Rife**—for proving that the new generation still has a backbone.

Keep speaking the truth. We're listening. And more importantly, we're laughing.

Because in a world that's trying to erase every sharp edge, laughter is the last rebellion we've got left.

Chapter 8:

Church, Hypocrisy, and Learning to See Through the Bullshit
Sunday Morning Theater

Before social media existed, there was church—the original performance platform. Same concept, different execution.

Everyone dressed in the best clothes, slapped on their holiest smile, and quietly judged the hell out of each other.

The gossip network ran on whispers and tactical side-eyes instead of likes and shares, but honestly? It was more efficient.

You knew who was broke, who was cheating, who'd been "sick" Sunday morning but fine enough for the casino Saturday night. The pews were your feed, the post-service parking lot was the comments section, and prayer requests were just group chats where secrets got weaponized with a side of "bless their heart."

I didn't grow up thinking I was too good for church or that I was some edgy rebel kid. I just learned to pay attention   probably the most un-Christian thing you can do in church. Church taught me to measure the Grand Canyon-sized gap between what people preached and how they actually lived.

That distance between words and actions became my real education. Everything I'd later see in politics, corporate boardrooms, and splattered all over the internet, I saw first in those wooden pews.

Turns out the best bullshit detector training doesn't cost $100K in college tuition—just a decade of Sunday mornings.

Growing Up Catholic in Southeast Texas

The church I attended was small and aggressively ordinary. Oil workers sat next to teachers; housewives chatted with retired cops. The place always smelled like old hymnals and coffee that had been burning since the Carter administration. Nothing fancy, nothing extreme—just regular people showing up on Sunday morning to maintain their eternal fire insurance policy.

How It Actually Worked

Looking the Part Mattered More
Than Being the Part.

Nobody rolled in wearing jeans unless they wanted to be the week's main prayer concern. Men wore suits that only saw daylight once a week, women wore dresses, kids wore whatever got ironed the night before while someone yelled about being late. If you showed up looking sloppy, people noticed and filed it away for later use. The logic went: if you can't bother to dress up for God, maybe you don't really care.

Never mind that God supposedly sees your heart—He apparently also has opinions about your shoe choices.

Always Say You're Fine
(Lying for Jesus).

When someone asked how you were doing, you said "blessed" or "living the dream" even if you were currently living the nightmare. Didn't matter if everything was falling apart. Your dog died, your bills were breeding in the mailbox, your marriage was held together with duct tape and spite—you still smiled and said you were fine. Admitting things were hard meant your faith was weak, which meant you were basically failing at Christianity. So, everyone performed their best lives. The real conversations happened later, in the parking lot, after most people left and the performance could finally end.

Money Talked Louder Than Prayers. The offering plate wasn't anonymous, no matter what they claimed. Those envelopes had numbers or names, and someone was absolutely keeping tabs like God's own accountant. Give too little and you'd get a friendly visit reminding you about the biblical importance of generosity (with percentages suggested). Win some money at the casino? I guarantee the priest would call to congratulate you and casually mention how God must want you to share that blessing with His house. They tracked finances harder than the IRS—except the IRS actually funds roads and schools instead of new stained glass nobody asked for.

Then came COVID. You couldn't go to church, but your money sure could—welcome to QR code tithing! The building was locked, but the Venmo was wide open. Funny how they filed for all that emergency government money to keep the church empty for a year or two. Turns out when push comes to shove, faith can be digital but rent can't.

Pick What You Like, Ignore the Rest (The Biblical Buffet)

The Bible got treated like a menu at Cheesecake Factory—overwhelmingly long, and everyone just picked their favorites. The church made a federal case about homosexuality but never mentioned that the same book condemned eating shellfish, wearing mixed fabrics, or getting tattoos. Guess which ones we actually followed? None of them, unless they were about other people.

We threw shrimp boils to raise money for church activities while preaching about biblical law with a straight face.

People used scripture like a Swiss Army knife—different tool for every situation. Someone got sick? "Gods got this, trust His plan!" That person died? "God called them home, praise Him!" Same book, same people, totally different messages depending on what made you feel better in the moment. Flexible theology for flexible times.

I was taught not to ask God for anything except forgiveness. Which, if you think about it, is a pretty sweet loophole. Steal the bike Monday, ask forgiveness Sunday, repeat. Turn the other cheek? Great, now I've got matching slap marks. Real practical stuff.

The People You'd Recognize Anywhere
The Rich Guy in the Front Row
(Mr. Spiritual Real Estate Mogul)

This man owned rental properties all over town and ran a used car lot that should've been investigated by several government agencies. Every Sunday he sat front and center, dressed like he had a personal meeting with God scheduled right after service. His suits probably cost more than most families made in a month. He made absolutely certain everyone watched him drop crisp hundred-dollar bills into the offering plate—probably the only time he ever gave anything without checking if it would appreciate in value.

What the congregation didn't see was him evicting families on Christmas Eve for being a day late on rent. Charging single mothers double for late fees. Selling cars with odometers rolled back further than his moral compass. But come Sunday, his money bought him respect and a front-row seat. The church cashed those checks and called him a pillar of the community. Turns out pillars can be built on pretty shaky foundations if they're expensive enough.

The lesson: Money doesn't make you clean. It just pays for better PR and a reserved parking spot.

The Woman Who Prayed About Everyone (The Prayer Warrior Gossip)

She never gossiped—perish the thought! She "shared prayer concerns." Totally different. Every week she'd corner you with fake sympathy dripping from her voice like holy water. "Oh sweetie, I've been *praying* for you. I heard about what's going on." Translation: "I know your business and I'm about to make it everyone else's business, but with Jesus involved so it's fine."

By the next day, half the church knew your private struggles because she'd put you on the prayer chain—which was basically a phone tree of sanctified gossip. Her specialty was other people's problems. Divorces, money troubles, teenagers who stopped showing up to youth group. She collected everyone's struggles like Pokémon cards and redistributed them as "concerns that need our prayers." She was basically running an intelligence operation, but with more casseroles.

The lesson: Sometimes the people praying the loudest are the ones doing the most damage. Amen.

The Humble Bragger
(The Anonymous Donor Who Needs Everyone to Know)

This guy couldn't stop mentioning his "anonymous" donations. Every conversation somehow boomeranged back to his charity work, his committee leadership, his servant's heart. "I don't do it for recognition," he'd say, right before making absolutely certain the pastor announced his latest contribution from the pulpit. You could always spot him during the announcement—he'd be the one standing up waving like he was in the Macy's Parade while everyone else sat confused about who this "anonymous" donor was.

Another dead giveaway: he'd slip his check into the offering plate late, after everyone else had already given, just to make sure maximum eyeballs witnessed his generosity. Timing is everything in performance art.

He loved quoting the part about how the left hand shouldn't know what the right hand is doing—while using both hands to applaud himself and possibly take a bow.

The lesson: When someone tells you how humble they are, they're not. Truly humble people don't have a PR strategy.

The Singer and Her Secrets
(The Angel with a Side Hustle)

She sang like an actual angel and lived like consequences were a myth. Every Sunday she'd perform "Amazing Grace" like it was written specifically for her redemption arc, then spend the rest of the week having affairs with married men from the Bible study group. You know, balancing the sacred and the profane.

People knew. They absolutely, 100% knew. But as long as she kept hitting those high notes, nobody said anything. Her husband sat three rows back, oblivious or in denial, clapping along with everyone else. "We all fall short," people would whisper, and then they'd go back to enjoying the free concert. Grace for me, judgment for thee, and show tunes for everyone.

The lesson: If you're talented enough, people will overlook almost anything. Star power works in church, too.

The Leaders We Trusted
(And Probably Shouldn't Have)

Then there were the priests and pastors. The ones who handled every important moment—weddings, baptisms, funerals, confessions. The same ones you modeled your life around, looked up to, trusted with your kids. Right up until you found out maybe that wasn't the best idea.

Stories circulated like communion wine. Youth ministers spending suspicious amounts of alone time with teenagers. Priests getting quietly reassigned to different parishes like a shell game with predators. Rumors that got buried faster than evidence before they could turn into facts. Files disappeared. People went on "sabbatical" and never came back.

I don't know if it happened in our specific church. I don't think it did. Maybe it was the church down the road, or two towns over. Hard to say when the evidence has a habit of vanishing and questions get treated like attacks on faith itself.

Meanwhile, these same people stood at the pulpit every week talking about purity, morality, and protecting children. And the collection plates kept filling up. The show must go on, I guess.

When the people meant to protect you become the potential threat, something fundamental breaks. Not always faith in God—but definitely faith in the institutions claiming to have His direct phone number.

The lesson: Authority doesn't equal trustworthiness. Titles are just words. Watch the actions.

When It Clicked

I was fifteen when I figured out that church wasn't really about God. It was about control, appearances, and maintaining the system. God was the branding. The product was conformity with a side of guilt.

What I Actually Learned

Look, church wasn't all terrible. I'm not going full super atheist here. It gave me a foundation, taught me about community, showed me that people can be genuinely kind when they stop worrying about appearances and actually act like the Jesus they claim to follow.

But the most valuable thing church taught me? How to spot bullshit from a mile away. It's like a superpower, but less cool.

I learned to watch what people *do* instead of listening to what they *say*. Actions over words. Results over rhetoric. Show me, don't tell me.

Now when a politician gets weepy about "protecting children" while cutting school lunch programs, I see the rich guy in the front row evicting families.

When a company changes their logo for Pride Month but donates to anti-LGBTQ candidates, I hear the Biblical buffet mentality—pick the parts that make you look good, ignore the inconvenient ones.

When an influencer talks about "authenticity" while their entire existence is a carefully curated, filtered, sponsored performance, I see Sunday morning theater—everyone's best self on display, reality saved for after the show.

Church didn't destroy my faith. It killed my willingness to take things at face value. In a world where everyone's selling something—salvation, progressive values, traditional family morals, protein powder—that's not a bad skill to have. Maybe it's the best skill.

We're All Playing the Same Game

Here's what I've figured out: everyone's a hypocrite sometimes. Me included. Every single one of us.

I've judged people for things I've done myself. I've criticized virtue signaling while carefully managing my own online image. I've rolled my eyes at performative activism while performing my own version of righteousness. We're all doing it, just with different audiences and different scripts.

The difference is—or at least what I'm *trying* for—is being honest about it. Not perfect, because perfect is boring and also impossible. Just honest.

That's what church could teach if it wanted to. Not how to fake it till you make it, but how to own your mistakes and actually grow. Not how to perform righteousness for the back row, but how to actually be decent when nobody's watching. Not how to look holy, but how to be human.

What Church Could Be

I don't go anymore. Haven't in years.

But I still think about what church *could* be. The idea of it, anyway. A place where people show up broken and leave feeling less alone instead of more judged. Where the money goes to feeding actual people instead of building bigger buildings with better sound systems. Where the message is about grace instead of guilt, about love instead of rules. Where everyone's actually welcome—not just people who look right, vote right, and dress right.

That version would matter. The kind where the pastor's hands are rough from real work, where people disagree but still eat together, where the sinners aren't just tolerated—they're expected, because we're all sinners and pretending otherwise is exhausting. A lot of "let me tell you about Jesus" energy, but actually backed up with "let me show you how Jesus did it" actions.

But like God, I don't think that church exists. Maybe it never did. Maybe it can't, because humans are involved and we're really good at screwing up good ideas.

Or maybe it's out there somewhere, small and quiet, doing the work without the performance. No stage lights, no front-row donors, no prayer chain gossip network.

I hope it exists. I just haven't found it yet.

And honestly? I'm not sure I'm looking that hard anymore.

Chapter 9:

The Year the Experts Died
The Dam Breaks

If I had to pick one year when ordinary people finally looked at "the experts" and said, "You've got to be kidding me," it would be 2020.

I'm not here to rehash every detail of the pandemic, every mandate, every statistic. You've already made up your mind on most of that, and so have I. What matters isn't the virus itself—it's what happened to trust. That's what died in 2020, and it's never coming back.

The institutions we were raised to respect—government, medicine, media, science—revealed themselves as fallible, political, and in some cases, flat-out dishonest. And when people noticed, when they pointed it out, they were told they were the problem.

That's when the experts lost us for good.

Essential vs. Expendable

Overnight, the country got divided into two groups: essential and non-essential.

On paper, "essential" sounded like an honor. In reality, it meant: if you stock shelves, drive trucks, work in a plant, fix power lines, or run a register, you don't get to stay home. You show up, virus or no virus.

Meanwhile, anyone who could work from a laptop stayed home, ordered delivery, and scolded everyone else on social media for "not taking it seriously enough."

The workers who kept the lights on, the food moving, the hospitals stocked—they weren't heroes. They were conscripted. And the people calling them heroes were the same ones having groceries delivered by those "essential" workers while tweeting "We're all in this together" from their kitchen islands.

We watched small businesses—family diners, gyms, barbershops—get shut down permanently. "Public health," they said.

Then we watched politicians who signed those orders get caught:

Eating at fancy restaurants with their masks off

Flying to vacation homes while telling everyone else to stay put

Getting haircuts in closed salons

Attending packed fundraisers after banning funerals

One governor told everyone to avoid gatherings, then got photographed at a birthday party in Napa Valley, indoors, unmasked, at a restaurant his own order had essentially shut down for regular people.

Another flew to Florida while his state froze and people died.

A mayor told citizens to stay home for Thanksgiving, then jetted off to Mexico.

People noticed. And they remembered.

The Science™ Kept Changing

For months, we were told to trust the science. Follow the experts. Listen to the authorities.

Then we watched those experts contradict themselves weekly:

Masks don't work. Masks are required. Two masks are better. Masks after vaccination. Masks forever. Masks off if you follow the "right" science.

The vaccine stops transmission. Well, it reduces transmission. Okay, it doesn't stop transmission but it keeps you out of the hospital. You'll need a booster. You'll need another booster. You'll need annual boosters.

Natural immunity doesn't count. Actually, it counts more than vaccination. Wait, we're not talking about natural immunity anymore.

Every press conference felt like someone was making it up as they went.

I'm not saying the experts should've known everything from day one. Real science is messy. Mistakes happen. Information changes.

But that's not how they sold it. They sold it as certainty. They sold it as settled. They told us to shut up and comply, then changed the rules three weeks later without apology or explanation.

People aren't stupid. They work jobs where being wrong gets someone hurt. They understand that if you don't know something, you say, "I don't know." You don't pretend you do, shame everyone who questions you, and then quietly change your story later.

The Censorship Machine

At the same time, Big Tech decided it knew better than everyone else.

Doctors with decades of experience got banned from platforms for asking questions. Scientists who disagreed with the official narrative got labeled "misinformation." Posts got flagged. Accounts got suspended. Videos got deleted.

You didn't have to be a conspiracy theorist to see what was happening. You just had to be paying attention.

The lab leak theory? Banned as misinformation. Then quietly admitted as possible a year later.

Questioning mask mandates for toddlers? Censored. Then multiple studies showed they did nothing.

Asking about vaccine side effects? Shut down as "anti-vax." Then the companies quietly added warnings to their packaging.

The message was clear: We'll tell you what's true. We'll tell you what questions you're allowed to ask. Sit down, shut up, and trust us.

But trust is earned, not demanded. And once you see the machinery of control, you can't unsee it.

Rules for Thee, Not for Me

We were told: no church, no weddings, no funerals, no visiting dying parents.

People said goodbye to loved ones over FaceTime. They watched funerals on Zoom. Some didn't even get that. They got a call from a nurse saying, "Your mother died alone. We'll send you, her things."

That's not a policy. That's cruelty with a clipboard.

But then summer came, and the streets filled with thousands of people. Shoulder to shoulder. Chanting, marching, sometimes burning. And suddenly, the same health officials who'd banned church services were signing letters saying these protests were okay.

Not just okay—necessary. Because racism, they said, is also a public health crisis.

So, ten people at a funeral? Super-spreader event.

Tens of thousands screaming in the streets? "An important expression of grief and anger."

You can support the protests. You can believe in their cause. But don't tell me the virus cared about the politics of the gathering. Either mass gatherings spread disease or they don't. The virus doesn't check your sign before it jumps.

That double standard—that blatant, in-your-face hypocrisy—is when millions of people quietly checked out. Not because they were anti-science. Because they were anti-bullshit.

The Experts Who Never Paid the Price

Here's what made it unbearable: the people making the rules never lived with the consequences.

The governor who shut down schools sent his own kids to private schools that stayed open.

The mayor who closed playgrounds was photographed at a packed beach.

The health official who said gyms were too dangerous had a home gym.

The politician who banned indoor dining was caught eating indoors.

They weren't in this with us. They were above it.

Meanwhile, the people who actually had to follow the rules were getting crushed:

Small business owners who'd spent their lives building something watched it die while big-box stores stayed open.

Parents tried to work from home while teaching their kids on Zoom.

Workers chose between a paycheck and their health.

Kids lost two years of normal childhood.

And when those people said, "This doesn't make sense," they were called selfish, ignorant, dangerous.

Not by the virus. By the people who never had to make those choices.

The Revolt Nobody Saw Coming

Something shifted in 2020 that the experts still don't understand.

People who'd spent their whole lives trusting institutions—teachers, doctors, government officials—started asking questions. Not because they became radicals. Because the answers stopped making sense.

Truck drivers, welders, nurses, teachers, parents—regular people who just wanted to live their lives—looked at the rules and said, "This is insane."

And when they said it out loud, they were told they were the problem. That they needed more education. That they needed to listen to their betters.

That condescension was the final straw.

Because here's the truth: the people who kept the country running in 2020 were the same people the experts looked down on. The "uneducated." The "deplorable." The ones who work with their hands and don't have advanced degrees.

Those people showed up every day while the laptop class lectured them from home about civic duty.

The New Rule of Thumb

If the people making the rules don't follow the rules, the rules aren't about safety. They're about control.

That's the lesson of 2020. Not that viruses are fake or that science is bad. That the people in charge will use any crisis to expand their power, and they'll wrap it in the language of concern while exempting themselves from every restriction they impose.

2020 didn't create distrust. It revealed it.

It showed us that:

The rules apply to some people and not others

The "experts" are often just politicians in lab coats

Questioning authority gets you labeled dangerous

The same people who demand your compliance never sacrifice anything themselves

The Experts Who Cried Wolf

The tragedy is that we actually need experts. We need doctors who know more than we do. We need scientists who can solve problems we don't understand. We need institutions we can trust when things go wrong.

But in 2020, those institutions spent all their credibility. They cashed in decades of trust for short-term compliance. And now, when they say "Trust us," people laugh.

That's not the public's fault. That's on them.

You don't rebuild trust by scolding people for not trusting you. You don't win credibility by censoring dissent. You don't earn respect by making rules you don't follow.

The experts died in 2020 not because they were wrong about everything. They died because they acted like being wrong didn't matter, and anyone who noticed was the enemy.

And here's the thing: they're still acting that way. Still expecting automatic deference. Still surprised when people roll their eyes.

They don't realize the spell is broken. The automatic trust is gone. And it's not coming back just because they want it to.

We learned our lesson. The question is: did they?

Chapter 10:

Dating When Romance Got an HR Department
The Old Deal

There used to be a script. Not written down, not debated in think pieces, not dissected in TikTok rants—just known. You learned it by watching your parents, your uncles, the couples at the diner who'd been holding hands for forty years. It wasn't perfect. It wasn't fair. But it worked.

Here's how it went:

Boy sees girl. Not on a screen. Not in a curated feed. In real life. At school. At church. At the grocery store, where she's reaching for the same box of cereal, and for one stupid second, the world narrows to the space between you and the Lucky Charms.

Boy gathers his courage. No texting. No sliding into DMs. No "Hey, what's up?" sent at 2 a.m. after three beers and a scroll through her Instagram. He walks up. He looks her in the eye. He says, "Can I take you to dinner?"

Girl decides. She says yes. She says no. Either way, she does it to his face, not to a phone screen. If she says no, he doesn't call her a bitch in a group chat. He doesn't screenshot her profile and post it in the "L's" thread. He nods, says "No problem," and moves on. Because rejection isn't trauma. It's just another chance to try again.

They go on a date. He picks her up. He opens the door. He pays—not because she's incapable, but because he's capable. They talk. They laugh. They argue about music or movies or whether pineapple belongs on pizza. They don't film it. They don't post it. They just live it.

They keep going or they don't. If it works, it works. If it doesn't, it doesn't. No ghosting. No breadcrumbing. No "We need to talk" texts at 1 a.m. that are really just "I'm bored and lonely but not lonely enough to commit." You break up, you shake hands, you move on. Or you don't break up at all. You get married. You have kids. You fight. You make up. You grow old together, and one day, your grandkids ask how you met, and you tell them about the cereal aisle.

That was the deal. It wasn't romantic. It was real.

The Gauntlet Was the Point

Dating wasn't supposed to be easy. That was the filter.

You didn't get to hide behind a screen. You didn't get to edit your flaws out of the story. You showed up—as you were, where you were—and if she liked it, great. If she didn't, well, there were other girls, other cereal aisles, other chances to get it right.

The stakes were higher, but so were the rewards.

You learned to talk to people. Not text. Not meme. Talk. Look them in the eye. Read their body language. Tell a joke and see if they actually laugh or just smile out of pity.

You learned to handle rejection. Not as a personal attack, but as a fact of life. "She's not into me" didn't mean "I'm worthless." It meant "Next."

You learned to commit. Because if you wanted her, you had to earn her. Flowers. Phone calls. Showing up. Not just when it was convenient, but when it was hard. When she was sick. When she was mad. When the newness wore off and all that was left was the choice to stay.

That's how you turned boys into men and girls into women. Not by swiping right, but by showing up.

The New Deal
(Or Lack Thereof)

Somewhere between dial-up and TikTok, the script got rewritten. Not by us. By algorithms. By corporations. By a culture that decided love was a product to be consumed, not a life to be built.

Now, the rules look like this:

Phase 1: The Illusion of Choice

You don't meet someone. You "match" with them. Based on an algorithm that knows you swiped right on brunettes who like hiking, but doesn't know you're terrified of commitment, still hung up on your ex, and only downloaded the app because your boys dared you to.

You don't ask her out. You "slide into her DMs" with a "Hey, what's up?" that she'll ignore because she gets fifty of those a day.

You don't plan a date. You "hang out." Which means you show up at her place with a six-pack and a Netflix password, and if you're lucky, you leave with more than a "We should do this again sometime" that you both know is a lie.

Phase 2: The Talking Stage

You text for weeks. Maybe months. You send memes. You analyze her "seen at" times. You overthink every "lol" and "ha-ha". You have deep conversations at 2 a.m. that you'd never dare have in person.

You are "exclusive" but not "official." You are "seeing each other" but not "dating." You are in a "situationship," which is just a "relationship" without the courage to call it that.

You meet her friends. You meet her dog. You do not meet her dad, because that would imply "serious," and "serious" is terrifying.

Phase 3: The Crash

One of you gets bored.

One of you gets clingy.

One of you sleeps with someone else.

One of you "isn't ready for a label."

One of you ghosts.

The other one spirals.

No closure. No handshake. Just a slow fade into "Who was that again?"

Who Killed Dating?

We did. Not on purpose. Not maliciously. We just let it happen. Here's how:

1. Smartphones Turned Flirting into a Team Sport

Before: You asked a girl out, and if she said no, only you and your boys knew.

Now: You ask a girl out, and if she says no, the entire group chat knows within five minutes. "Bro, she left you on read. LMAO." "Dude, you got the blue check? That's rough, king."

Result: Men stopped asking. Women stopped saying yes. Now, everyone's too scared to make a move.

2. Porn Taught Men to Want a Fantasy

Before: You learned about sex from awkward conversations, stolen Playboys, and trial and error with a girl who was just as clueless as you.

Now: You learn about sex from Pornhub, where women are always eager, always perfect, and always leave before the awkward "So... was that good for you?" conversation.

Result: Real women—with their moods, their boundaries, their humanity—can't compete. So, men either opt out entirely or treat sex like a transaction. "Why buy the cow when the milk is free?" Except now, the milk is endless, and the cow is a myth.

3. Feminism Got Hijacked by Corporations

Before: Women wanted respect. Men wanted to provide. It wasn't perfect, but there was a balance.

Now: Women are told "You don't need a man!"—then shamed when they admit they're lonely. Men are told "Be a gentleman!"—then called "toxic" when they pay for dinner. Everyone's confused, everyone's angry, and nobody's happy.

Result: Dating isn't a partnership. It's a power struggle. And when love becomes a battle, everybody loses.

4. Social Media Turned Love into Content

Before: Your relationship was private. Your fights stayed between you. Your breakups were your business.

Now: Your relationship is a "couple goals" post. Your fights are subtweets. Your breakup is a "single king/queen" era. Everything is performative. Nothing is real.

Result: People would rather look happy than be happy. And when the performance ends, they're left with nothing but likes and an empty bed.

5. Fear of Consequences Made Cowards of Us All

Before: If you messed up, you apologized. If you hurt someone, you owned it. If you were wrong, you fixed it.

Now: One wrong word and you're "canceled." One bad date and you're a "red flag." One mistake and your name is in a group chat with "Yikes" and "Block him."

Result: Nobody takes risks. Nobody puts in effort. Nobody dares to love, because love requires vulnerability, and vulnerability is the most dangerous thing in the world.

The Fallout: A Generation That Doesn't Know How to Love
The Numbers Don't Lie

Men under 30 are having less sex than any generation in history. Not because they don't want to, but because they don't know how. Porn and video games don't require rejection. Why risk it?

Women under 30 are the loneliest demographic in America. They're told they "Don't need a man," but nobody told them how to want one without feeling weak.

Marriage rates are plummeting. Not because people don't believe in love, but because they don't believe in themselves. If you can't handle a bad date, how are you going to handle a bad marriage?

Dating apps are a $3 billion industry. And what are they selling? Not love. Addiction. The next swipe. The next match. The next hit of "Maybe this one will fix me."

The Stories We Tell Ourselves

"I'm not ready for a relationship." (Translation: "I'm terrified of failing at one.")

"I'm focusing on my career." (Translation: "I'd rather be safe than happy.")

"I just haven't met the right person." (Translation: "I refuse to commit to anyone who might disappoint me.")

"I'm happy single." (Translation: "I've given up.")

How to Bring It Back
(If We Even Want To)

Dating isn't dead. It's just hiding. Buried under algorithms, fear, and the lie that love should be easy. If you want it back, here's how to dig it up:

For Men:

Put the phone down.

You don't need her Snapchat score to know if she's worth your time. Look her in the eye. Ask her out. In person.

Be a man, not a meme.

Open doors. Pay for dinner. Not because she's helpless, but because you're capable. Chivalry isn't dead—it's just been rebranded as "toxic." Ignore the noise.

Handle rejection like a grown-up.

She said no? "Cool. Have a good one." No arguments. No guilt trips. No "But why?" texts. Move on.

Stop watching porn.

It's not "harmless fun." It's rewiring your brain to want something that doesn't exist. Real women have stretch marks, bad days, and opinions. Learn to love that.

For Women:

Let him lead.

If he asks you out, say "Yes" or "No." Don't say "Maybe" or "Let's just hang out." If you want a man, act like a woman who wants a man, not one who's auditioning for a Netflix special.

Stop testing him.

"Prove you're not like the others" is a game no one wins. If he's worth your time, he'll show you. If he's not, next.

Don't sleep with him on the first date.

I don't care if that makes me "old-fashioned." Sex is the glue, not the foundation. Build something worth sticking to first.

Stop dating boys.

If he's still playing video games at 28, if his idea of a date is "Netflix and chill," if he can't hold a conversation without his phone, he's not a man. Walk away.

For Both of Us:

Delete the apps.

You're not "exploring your options." You're avoiding commitment. If you want love, act like it.

Go where real people are.

Churches. Coffee shops. Volunteer events. Anywhere that isn't a bar or a club. Love doesn't happen in the comments section.

Stop treating dating like a job interview.

You're not "vetting" a life partner. You're getting to know a person. Relax. Have fun. If it's meant to be, it'll be.

Fight for it.

Love isn't "easy." It's worth it. If you're not willing to work, you don't deserve the reward.

The Truth No One Wants to Admit

We don't have a "dating problem." We have a courage problem.

We'd rather swipe than risk rejection. We'd rather ghost than have a hard conversation. We'd rather perform than be real.

But here's the secret: The people who are truly happy in love? They're not special. They're just brave.

Brave enough to ask. Brave enough to fail. Brave enough to try again.

So put down the phone. Walk up to someone. Ask them out.

And if they say no?

Next.

Final Thought: Love isn't dead. But it's waiting for you to show up. Will you?

Chapter 11:

Marriage, Sex, and the Day
"I Do" Came with a Prenup and a Safe Word
The Marriage Contract of 1995:
No Lawyers, No Loopholes

Back in the day, marriage wasn't a negotiation. It was a hostage situation—and everybody signed up willingly.

The rules were simple, unwritten, and enforced by your mama's wooden spoon:

Man's Job: Bring home the bacon, fix the leaky faucet, and occasionally scare off the neighbor's creepy cousin who lingered a little too long at the barbecue.

Woman's Job: Keep the house from burning down (literally and metaphorically), raise the kids to not be felons, and remind her husband that "no, you cannot wear that shirt to your sister's wedding."

Sex: Frequent, enthusiastic, and the primary reason you didn't murder each other over who left the toilet seat up.

Duration: "Till death do us part" wasn't a suggestion. It was a threat. You stayed. You figured it out. You didn't have time for midlife crises because you were too busy paying off the minivan.

Nobody pretended it was easy. Nobody claimed it was fair. But it was clear. You weren't signing up for a trial period. You were signing up for life—like a gym membership, but with way more screaming and slightly better benefits.

Sex Ed, 1990s Style:
No Pamphlets, Just Trauma

We didn't learn about sex from YouTube tutorials or TikTok influencers. We learned it from:

Our parents' bedroom door, which was always closed after 10 p.m., accompanied by the unmistakable sound of a box spring that had seen better days.

Dad grabbing Mom's butt in the kitchen when he thought we weren't looking (we were always looking).

The fact that they fought like cats and dogs—but still slept in the same bed every night, because "separate beds" was what old people and TV characters did.

Nobody handed us a "Healthy Relationships" worksheet. We figured it out the old-fashioned way: awkwardly, clumsily, and with a 50/50 chance of someone getting elbowed in the face.

You had to look your wife in the eye the next morning over Folgers and stale donuts, so you tried to get it right. And if you didn't? Well, she'd let you know—usually by throwing a shoe at your head or "accidentally" burning your favorite T shirt.

Then the Internet Showed Up and Ruined Everything

Fast forward to today, and the marriage contract has been rewritten by people who think "commitment" is a Wi-Fi password. Here's what changed:

1. Porn:
The World's Worst Sex Ed Teacher

Before: You learned about sex from actual women—who had opinions, moods, and the occasional yeast infection.

Now: Boys learn about sex from Pornhub, where women are always eager, always hairless, and never say "Not tonight, honey, I have a migraine."

Result: A generation of men who think sex should come with a mute button and a "skip intro" option. Then they get married, try to reenact their favorite scene, and wonder why their wife is crying instead of moaning.

2. No-Fault Divorce:
The Ultimate "Take-Backsies"

Before: Divorce was messy, expensive, and socially unacceptable unless your spouse was actually a serial killer.

Now: Divorce is as easy as canceling a gym membership—except the gym doesn't take half your stuff and your kids.

Result: People treat marriage like a Netflix subscription— "If I don't like it after two seasons, I'll just cancel."

3. Dating Apps:
The All-You-Can-Eat
Buffet of Regret

Before: You dated someone from your town, your church, or your workplace. If you broke up, you still had to see them at the grocery store. Accountability, baby.

Now: You can swipe through potential partners like a menu at Cheesecake Factory. "Eh, she's cute, but what if someone better comes along?"

Result: A generation of people who can't commit to a lunch order, let alone a lifetime.

4. Social media:
The Ex-Olympics

Before: If you broke up, you avoided your ex like the plague. If you ran into them, you nodded politely and kept walking.

Now: You can stalk your ex's new relationship in real time, complete with vacation photos, couple's workouts, and the inevitable "We're so blessed!" posts that make you want to drink bleach.

Result: Nobody moves on. Everybody's bitter. And your therapist is buying a second yacht.

5. Therapy Culture: Just Follow Your Heart (But Also, Here's a Bill)"

Before: You stayed together "for the kids" because somebody had to raise them, and it sure as hell wasn't going to be the state.

Now: Therapists and influencers tell you "You deserve to be happy!"—as if happiness is a permanent state and not a fleeting emotion that disappears the second your Wi-Fi cuts out.

Result: People bail at the first sign of trouble, then wonder why their third marriage is just as miserable as the first two.

The Numbers Don't Lie
(But We Pretend They Do)

Here's the funny thing: Married people are still winning.

Married couples have more sex—and better sex—than single people. (Yes, even after kids. No, I don't know how either.)

Married men live longer, make more money, and are less likely to die alone in a nursing home while a nurse steals their painkillers.

Married women report higher life satisfaction than their single counterparts—even when they're the ones doing 70% of the emotional labor.

Yet we're told marriage is "outdated," "oppressive," and "a trap."

Meanwhile, single people in their 20s and 30s are having so little sex that researchers had to invent a new category: "Sexless Young Adults." One in four under 30 didn't have sex once last year. But sure, let's keep pretending that sleeping around is the path to happiness.

What Porn Stole
(Besides Your Dignity)

Porn didn't just give men unrealistic expectations about body types. It gave them unrealistic expectations about sex itself.

No conversation required. (Real women talk. Sometimes during. Deal with it.)

No rejection. (Real women say "no." Sometimes "hell no." Learn to take it like a man.)

No morning breath. (Real women wake up looking like they survived a hurricane. Love her anyway.)

No pregnancy scares. (Real sex has consequences. Wear a condom like a grown-up.)

Then these guys get married and discover that real women have:

Moods (not just the "ready to go" kind).

Periods (yes, blood. No, you can't opt out).

Jobs (she's not just "the hot one" from your fantasies—she's a person).

Opinions (and she will use them).

Suddenly, the guy who spent his 20s watching "step-sister" videos can't perform without a second screen. That's not freedom. That's a prison with bad lighting.

What "You Go, Girl!" Really Meant

Women were sold a bill of goods, too.

"You don't need a man!"

(Cool. Who's changing the tire at midnight in the rain?)

"Career first, kids later!"

(Great. Now you're 40, infertile, and your eggs cost more than your 401k.)

"Sleep with whoever you want!"

(Awesome. Now you're wondering why none of them stick around for breakfast.)

Here's the truth: You can have it all. Just not all at once. And not if you spend your 20s treating men like they're disposable, then get mad when they return the favor in your 30s.

You can be a boss at work and still want your man to take charge in bed. You can be independent and still let him carry the heavy stuff. You can demand respect and still make him feel needed.

Wanting both doesn't make you weak. It makes you human.

The Marriages That Still Work
(And Why They're Pissing Off the Internet)

I know plenty of couples thriving in 2025. Their secret? They're doing it the old-fashioned way.

They have sex. A lot. Even when tired. Especially when mad. (Nothing solves an argument like a well-timed grope in the kitchen.)

They don't air their fights on TikTok. (The world does not need to see your husband's midlife crisis play out in 60-second clips.)

They don't keep score. (No chore charts. No orgasm tally sheets. If you're counting, you're losing.)

One leads, the other follows—without turning it into a UN summit. (Someone's got to make the call. Flip a coin if you have to.)

Divorce isn't an option, so they fix problems instead of threatening to leave. (Because "I could just leave" is the relationship equivalent of "I could just jump out of this moving car.")

No kink contracts. No spreadsheets. Just two people who decided the grass isn't greener—it's AstroTurf, and it's full of dog crap.

A Message to Married Men:
Stop Being a Child

Gentlemen, your wife chose you. Out of billions of men on this planet, she picked you. Act like it.

Work like her life depends on your paycheck. (Because it does.)

Lift heavy stuff. Kill spiders. Change the tire in the rain. (Yes, even if she can do it herself. Let her watch you do it.)

Stand between her and anything that scares her. (Including her own bad decisions.)

Then come home, shower, grab her in the kitchen, and take her to bed like you're still trying to win her. (Because you are.)

She will follow you through hell if she knows you'd burn the world down to keep her safe.

A Message to Married Women:
Stop Mothering Your Husband

Ladies, he's not your project. He's your partner.

Let him be a man. (If he puts the toilet paper roll on backward, let it go.)

Stop correcting him in front of the kids. (Undermine him at home, and he'll stop leading anywhere.)

**If he wants sex and you're not in the mood, say "Not tonight"—not "Ugh, fine." (Nothing kills desire faster than obligation.)

Treat him like your husband, not your girlfriend with a paycheck. (He'll move mountains for you if you let him.)

To the Single People: Stop Swiping and Start Building

If all you want is endless casual sex, fine. Own it. But don't act shocked when you're 35, your cat is your only roommate, and your right hand is your most committed relationship.

If you want the real thing—kids, legacy, someone who's seen you puke and still kisses you goodnight—stop treating dating like a buffet.

Date like it's 1995. (Ask her out. In person. With words.)

Court like your grandpa did. (Flowers. Dinners. Effort.)

Save sex for someone who deserves it. (If he's not willing to wait, he's not willing to stay.)

Marry someone you'd be proud to grow old and fat with. (Because everybody gets old and fat. The question is: Who's still going to laugh with you about it?)

The Bottom Line:
We Broke It, We Can Fix It

We turned sex into a sport, marriage into a contract, and love into a feeling that expires when the Wi-Fi cuts out. Then we act shocked when half of marriages explode and the other half limp along in separate bedrooms, communicating only through passive-aggressive Post-it notes.

Here's the truth:

God, biology, or common sense—pick your flavor—designed men and women to fit together. Like puzzle pieces. Like locks and keys. Like peanut butter and jelly.

When we stop fighting that design and start working with it, everything else falls into place.

The marriage bed is still the cheapest therapy, the best gym, and the strongest glue a man and woman will ever find.

Everything else? Noise.

So, turn off the phone. Lock the door. And prove me wrong.

Chapter 12:

When We Had Room for Everybody
(And Didn't Need a Rulebook)
The Way Things Were

I grew up in a time when people didn't fit neatly into boxes—and nobody much cared. We didn't have committees, hashtags, or HR departments policing how we talked, thought, or lived. We had something better: common sense, live-and-let-live, and the understanding that not everybody had to be the same to belong.

There was Sam.

Sam was the kind of girl who could out-throw, out-cuss, and out-drink half the boys in our town. She wore flannel shirts, worked on cars, and had a laugh that could shake the rafters of a barn. She was what folks used to call a tomboy—a girl who didn't much care for dresses or dolls but wasn't trying to be a boy, either. She was just Sam.

And that was fine.

Nobody demanded she pick a side. Nobody insisted we call her "he" or pretend she was something she wasn't. She didn't need our approval—she just needed us to leave her alone. And we did.

She wanted to work on engines, drink beer with the guys, and be treated like one of the crew. So that's what we did. No big speeches. No identity crises. No social media campaigns. She was who she was, and the world kept spinning.

That's how it worked back then.

Jason and the Barbie Phase

Then there was Jason.

Jason was the kind of kid who'd rather play with his sister's Barbies than our GI Joes. We teased him—kids are cruel, and the '90s were no exception—but it wasn't some grand moral outrage. It was just kids being kids. He took it in stride, grew up, got married, had a couple of boys, and now coaches their football team.

A total 180 from the kid who used to braid dolls' hair.

Nobody told him he was "actually a girl." Nobody suggested he needed hormones or surgery. He just... grew up. Found his place. Moved on.

Because back then, we had room for people to just be.

The Quiet Understanding

We had all kinds in our little town:

Tomboys who stayed women—no identity crises, no demands for new pronouns, just girls who liked dirt bikes and didn't see the point in makeup.

Sensitive boys who became men—guys who cried at movies, wrote poetry, and still knew how to swing a hammer.

Gay folks who lived their lives—some quiet, some loud, but none of them insisting the rest of us rewrite reality to make them comfortable.

There was space. Not because we were enlightened, but because we were busy living. We didn't have time to turn every personal quirk into a political statement. If you were weird, fine. If you were quiet, fine. If you were loud, fine. Just don't make it everybody else's problem.

And it wasn't.

The New Rules:
Sharper Teeth, Less Mercy

Now?

Now a girl who hates dresses gets told she's "Actually a boy" before she's old enough to drive.

Now a boy who likes dolls gets fast-tracked to hormone shots by adults who should know better.

Now a stranger on the internet can destroy your life if you call them "sir" instead of "xer."

This isn't freedom. It's a new rulebook—one with harsher penalties than the old one ever had.

What Changed?

We Used to Let People Be. Now We Demand **They Perform**.

Before: "That's just how Sam is." (Shrug.)

Now: "You MUST affirm, celebrate, and financially support Sam's journey or you're a bigot!"

Kids Used to Grow Out of Phases. Now They Get Locked into Them.

Before: Jason played with Barbies, then grew up and had sons who play football.

Now: If a boy likes pink, he's "trans" by lunch and on puberty blockers by dinner.

We Used to Mind Our Own Business. Now Everybody's a Cop.

Before: "Not my kid, not my problem."

Now: "You didn't clap loud enough for my pronouns! Reported!"

Dissent Used to Be Tolerated
Now It's a Career-Ending Crime.

Before: "Eh, agree to disagree."

Now: "WRONG. YOU ARE NOW UNEMPLOYABLE."

The Cost of the New Orthodoxy

We've traded live-and-let-live for comply-or-be-destroyed.

Parents are terrified their kids will get **brainwashed** in school.

Teachers are afraid to say "boys and girls" lest they get **fired.**

Kids are growing up confused, not because they're different, but because adults keep telling them they are.

Regular people are walking on eggshells, wondering if today's the day they lose everything for using the wrong word.

And for what?

For the **illusion of progress**—while real people suffer in silence.

The Way Forward:
Common Sense in a World Gone Mad

We don't need new rules. We need the old understanding:

1. Let People Be
(Without Making It Your Job to "Fix" Them)

If Sam wants to wear flannel and work on cars, let her.

If Jason wants to play with dolls, let him.

If your uncle's gay, let him be gay.

But don't demand the rest of us pretend reality isn't real.

2. Stop Medicalizing Childhood

Boys who like pink are not "girls."

Girls who hate dresses are not "boys."

Kids go through phases. Let them.

3. Mind Your Own Business

Not your kid? Not your problem.

Not your body? Not your say.

Not your life? Then butt out.

4. Bring Back the Art of Disagreeing
Without Destroying Each Other

"I don't see it that way, but it's a free country."

"You do you, man."

"Live and let live."

ROGER MONARCH JR.

The Truth Nobody Wants to Admit

We didn't used to need all these rules because we had something better: trust.

We trusted that people would figure themselves out without a committee meeting.

We trusted that kids would grow up without being permanently altered by adults with agendas.

We trusted that being different didn't mean being broken.

Now?

Now we've replaced trust with control, freedom with fear, and common sense with dogma.

And the worst part?

The people who suffer the most aren't the activists—they're the regular folks just trying to live their lives.

Final Thought: What We Lost
(And How to Get It Back)

We didn't used to need a movement for everything because we had something simpler:

Room.

Room for Sam to be Sam. Room for Jason to grow up. Room for people to be who they were without a parade or a protest.

We can have that again.

But first, we have to stop letting the loudest voices drown out the rest of us.

Stop obeying the new rulebook.

And start living like free people again.

Question for the Road: When did we decide that the only way to be kind was to lie? And when are we going to stop?

Timeout
or
Intermission
Fair Warning

Alright, folks, this is the chapter where half of you are going to slam this book shut like it's a spider in your cereal box. The other half are going to nod so hard you'll need a chiropractor. A few of you will clutch your pearls in public but DM me later with "Finally, someone said it!" Either way—grab some popcorn. This is where things get fun.

First, let's set the mood. If you're a chicken reading this—relax. None of this applies to you. You're just here for the corn. If you're a banana reading this—please put the book down. You've been through enough already. Frankly, I'm amazed you can read. But if you must continue, imagine Morgan Freeman's voice narrating this to you. Better? Good. Now we can proceed.

Here's your friendly neighborhood truth bomb:

I'm about to stop gently lowering you into the pool and instead throw you into the deep end like an unwanted pool floatie.

Here it is, plain and simple:

I don't buy into the gender-identity-pronoun circus.

I believe you're born male or female. Period. Not a spectrum. Not a buffet. Not a Build-A-Bear workshop where you stuff yourself with whatever identity feels coziest that moment.

I don't believe in swapping body parts like you're playing Operation after three tequila shots.

Call me old-fashioned. Call me a dinosaur. Call me "Sir"—I've been called worse by people I respect more.

That's how I was raised. That's what I believe. And I'm not apologizing for it.

(Pause for dramatic effect. Sip your drink. Take a deep breath.)

Notice something missing from that statement?

I didn't say you can't believe differently.

I didn't demand you be fired.

I didn't call for a boycott of your Etsy shop.

I didn't threaten to report you to HR because your worldview gives me hives.

Remember when we could disagree over dinner and still share a plate of ribs without stabbing each other with the fork? Pepperidge Farm remembers.

Look, if you believe there are 97 genders and people can switch between them based on Mercury being in retrograde or how their horoscope feels that morning—mazel tov. You do you. Live your best life. I'm not camped outside bathrooms with a clipboard and a scowl.

But here's the thing:

My beliefs? They still count too.

They still matter. They're still allowed—even if Twitter forgot that part of the First Amendment.

You can:

Hate me for this

Keep reading because you're morbidly curious

Slam this book shut and write a 1-star review with enough angry emojis to make a Gen Z'er proud

Either way, thanks for sticking around this long.

Still here? Excellent. You're my kind of people.

Let's keep going—because things are about to get really interesting.

(Cue dramatic chipmunk music)

Chapter 13:

When Words Became a Trap
The Old Rules

Let me get this straight: If you're an adult just trying to live your life—gay, straight, trans, purple with polka dots—I don't care. Wear what you want, love who you love, cut your hair into a mohawk or shave it all off. My only hope for you is that you find some happiness in this mess of a world.

I've worked alongside gay folks my entire life. Never had a problem. Back in the day, I misgendered butch lesbians all the time—short hair, flannel shirts, work boots, that deep voice that made you do a double-take. I'd say "Yes, sir," and they'd either laugh, correct me, or just keep talking like it never happened. I'd turn beat red, mumble an apology, and that was that. No drama. No HR meetings. Just life moving on.

Same as the time I asked a woman at the grocery store when she was due—only to realize she wasn't pregnant. I wanted the floor to open up and swallow me whole. Embarrassing? Absolutely. The end of the world? Not even close. Nobody filmed it. Nobody demanded I attend sensitivity training. We just exchanged an awkward laugh and went about our day.

But here's where I draw the line: When someone demands I say things I know aren't true.

When I'm told I have to deny what my own eyes see. When reality is supposed to bend because someone updated their Instagram bio. That's not kindness. That's not progress. That's a shakedown with a rainbow flag draped over it.

And I learned that lesson the hard way on a slow weekday afternoon in a half-empty restaurant.

The Pronoun Ambush

I was managing the place that day. Just a few regulars nursing their coffee, the hum of the AC fighting against the Texas heat. Then in walked two kids in their mid-twenties. One of them looked like they'd gotten dressed by throwing a blindfolded dart at a thrift store rack—baggy, mismatched clothes, hair that looked like it had lost a fight with a weed whacker. Nothing about them screamed "man" or "woman." Just "I gave up and grabbed whatever was clean-ish."

They ate. They paid. And when I handed over the receipt, I said, "Here you go, ma'am." Pure habit. Pure Southeast Texas reflex.

That's when the fireworks started.

"MA'AM?!" The kid shot up like I'd just announced the apocalypse. "I use HE/HIM pronouns!"

I blinked. I knew what pronouns were—I wasn't raised in a cave—but I'd never heard someone announce their preferred grammar like it was a life-or-death medical condition. Confused, I asked, "What exactly are you using them for?"

Big mistake.

Their friend jumped in like an overcaffeinated bouncer. "They identify as a man."

They? Identify? My brain short-circuited. I thought maybe this was a joke. We pulled pranks on each other all the time at work. Hell, I once tried to hire a male stripper for a buddy's birthday without him knowing—pure comedy gold.

So, I asked, "Is this a joke? That's why you dressed like that?"

The first kid stepped closer, chin jutting out like they were about to throw down. "I'm more of a man than you'll ever be."

I forced a smile. "Okay, buddy. You, them, they, whoever—have a great day." I turned to walk away.

But they weren't done. "You better wake up." More posturing. More declarations of superior masculinity. The exact words are fuzzy, but the sentiment was clear: I am manlier than you, and you will acknowledge it.

151

By now, the whole restaurant had gone quiet. Customers watching. Cooks peeking through the kitchen pass. I could feel my temper rising—not because I wanted to fight, but because I recognized the script. This wasn't about a mistake. This was performance art with an audience.

I looked that kid dead in the eye and said, "You're a man right up until you get your ass whipped. Then when the cops show up, you'll be a woman again. An ugly one."

Silence.

I walked away, pissed. They stormed out. I figured that was the end of it.

One of the waitresses muttered, "I hope this doesn't end up on TikTok." It didn't—at least not the actual incident—but some twisted version of the story got narrated by what looked like Gollum's long-lost sister across every platform she could find.

Two days later, I got the call from corporate. Not fired—yet—but I was sentenced to four hours of "sensitivity training." Me and four other unfortunate souls in a beige room while a trainer clicked through PowerPoint slides about pronouns, safe spaces, and microaggressions. The trainer—who clearly wanted to be anywhere else—kept rolling his eyes and muttering, "Look, I know this is bullshit, but it's policy." He said it at least six times. The whole message was clear: It doesn't matter if it makes sense. It doesn't matter if you believe it. Policy says swallow it or get out.

I walked out of there not one bit more "sensitive," but a whole lot more convinced that this had nothing to do with protecting people and everything to do with control.

The Friend I Lost

This is where I lost a friend I'd known since we were kids.

Let's call him Jeff. We grew up together. Watched each other's kids come into the world. His boys were wild—no discipline, no structure—but that was his business, not mine.

One night, we're sitting on his porch, and he tells me one of his sons is now his "daughter." Without thinking, I said, "Man, you should've whipped his ass more when he was little."

Jeff's face went stone cold. "I'd never say something like that about your kids."

I shot back, "Wouldn't have needed to. Mine would've never pulled that stunt."

I could've chosen different words. I could've just kept my mouth shut. But I didn't.

And just like that, a friendship that had lasted decades died on that porch.

We still nod at each other when we run into each other. If he needed help, I'd give it. I'm sure he'd do the same. But something broke that night.

Jeff went all in—Proud Parent shirts, new flags, the whole social media performance. He got love from strangers and side-eye from people who actually knew him. The last post I saw before he deleted his Facebook—or blocked his real-life friends—was someone asking, "Proud parent—are you even you anymore, Jeff?"

I didn't write it. I don't do that kind of thing online. But the wall was up.

Was I too harsh? Probably. Do I lie awake wishing I'd sugarcoated it? Sometimes. But I'm not going to stand there and lie about what I believe just to keep the peace. That's the price you pay for honesty. Some days it feels worth it. Some days you sit alone with a beer and wonder.

The Bathroom Showdown

About a year later, I stopped by a bar I used to run. Before my burger even hit the table, I heard yelling near the restrooms. Same type of character—screaming at a nineteen-year-old waitress about needing a "gender-neutral bathroom" in a fifty-year-old dive with two stalls and plumbing that barely worked on a good day.

This was in a town where that kind of demand just doesn't happen. When it does, it's always dramatic, always loud, and there's usually a camera involved. (I learned that in sensitivity training.)

The poor kid behind the counter kept saying, "I'm sorry, but we only have two bathrooms. I can't change the building." But this wasn't about plumbing. It was about power.

The Nightclub Days

See, back in the early 2000s, I owned a nightclub. Not some dive bar—a real club. Three rooms, three DJs, electronic music, rave parties every weekend. We'd pack 3,000 people in there on a good night.

And you saw everything.

Guys in full makeup. Girls dressed like guys. People in costumes that defied description—glow sticks, body paint, platform boots, outfits that made Vegas showgirls look modest. Some of them barely looked human, let alone male or female.

And you know what we never had a problem with?

Bathrooms.

Three thousand people a night. Some of them barely recognizable as male or female. Some going by names like Starlight, Neon, Volt—names they made up for the weekend.

But they all knew which bathroom to use.

Mike, dressed head-to-toe in sequins with a wig down to his waist? Men's room. David, wearing more eyeliner than most women I knew? Men's room. The woman who called herself "Raven" and looked like she'd walked off the set of The Matrix? Women's room.

Nobody argued. Nobody demanded a third option. Nobody threw a fit. Nobody needed a corporate memo.

Because even in the most alternative, anything-goes space you could imagine, people still understood basic reality.

They weren't pretending to be something they weren't. They were expressing themselves. Having fun. Pushing boundaries. Living out fantasies.

But they weren't demanding that I—or anyone else—deny what we all could see with our own eyes.

Monday Morning Reality

Here's the kicker:

Come Monday morning, most of those people went back to their regular lives.

They put on suits. Went to offices. Answered phones. Filed reports. Sat in cubicles. And nobody at work knew they'd spent Saturday night covered in glitter with a wig down to their waist.

They didn't bring their weekend personas to the office. Didn't demand coworkers use their rave names. Didn't file HR complaints because someone said "sir" instead of "Starlight."

They didn't need the whole world to validate who they were on the weekend.

They lived their lives. Let other people live theirs. And everybody got along just fine.

Back to the Bar

I took another sip of my beer and watched the guy still arguing with the waitress about the bathroom.

And it hit me: **This is different.**

The people at my club? They wanted to be different. To stand out. To escape the ordinary for a night.

This guy? He didn't want to be different.

He wanted to be validated. He wanted to be seen. He wanted every person in that bar to stop what they were doing and acknowledge him.

He wasn't there to use the bathroom. He was there to start a fight.

I'd seen this before. These people go into businesses, restaurants, bars—anywhere with employees too scared to push back—and they look for conflict. They pick the youngest, most nervous worker they can find. Someone trained to apologize for existing.

And they start an argument they know the employee can't win.

They ask impossible questions. Make unreasonable demands. And they record it all.

Not because they're facing real discrimination. Not because they actually care about the bathroom.

Because they want the confrontation. The video. The clicks. The attention.

Just like what happened to me.

At my club, we had 3,000 people a night who just wanted to dance and have fun.

At that bar, we had one guy who wanted to be a victim.

And that's the difference.

I watched that poor kid—nineteen, maybe twenty—getting chewed out for something completely out of his control.

I'd had enough.

The Line in the Sand

I turned on my barstool and said—loud enough for the whole room to hear—

"We don't need a gender-neutral bathroom."

The guy froze mid-rant and stared at me like I'd just materialized out of thin air.

I kept going.

"If you've got nuts, use the men's room. If you don't, use the women's. Problem solved. Everybody in the world falls into one of those two categories. You either have 'em or you don't."

Dead silence.

The guy looked at me like I'd just slapped his mother.

Then, without a word, he turned and walked out.

The waitress behind the bar let out a breath like she'd been holding it for hours. A couple of customers started clapping. Some guy I'd never met bought me a beer. The manager came over, shook my hand, and said, "Dinner's on the house tonight."

And in that moment, I realized something I'd suspected for a while but never fully understood until then:

I wasn't the only one sick of this.

The Lesson

Every person in that bar had been thinking the same thing I said. They just couldn't say it.

Because they were employees. Because they had policies to follow. Because they were afraid of getting fired, or reported, or turned into the next viral villain.

That waitress knew the guy was full of it. The manager knew it. The customers knew it.

But nobody could say it.

Except me.

Because I didn't work there anymore. I didn't have a corporate office breathing down my neck. I didn't have an HR department monitoring my every word.

I was just a guy having a beer.

And I said what everybody else was thinking.

And nothing happened to me.

No sensitivity training. No write-ups. No viral mob coming after me.

Just a free meal, a handshake, and the quiet understanding that I wasn't alone in being tired of the nonsense.

Somewhere along the way, we stopped being able to just live and let live. Now, every word is a test. Every interaction is a potential minefield. Every mistake is a career-ending offense.

But that night in the bar, for just a moment, it felt like the old way again.

And that's worth more than all the sensitivity training in the world.

Chapter 14:

When Corporations Bought Virtue
Pride Before the Logos

There was a time when Pride was simple. It was a parade in a big city or a date on a calendar. If you were gay and wanted to go, you went. If you weren't, you stayed home. Nobody cared. There was no company scorecard or HR reminder to "participate."

It wasn't a marketing tool. It wasn't a social media campaign. It lived in quiet bars with the windows blacked out. It lived in marches where people risked losing jobs, friends, and sometimes their lives. They weren't after likes or brand deals. They were just tired of hiding.

That brave version of Pride belonged to people. Now it belongs to corporations that learned there's money in virtue.

The Month-Long Performance

By the mid-2010s, something shifted. June stopped being a month and became a ritual. Rainbow logos appeared like clockwork. Every major brand suddenly discovered they'd been allies all along.

In October I can go into a store to buy cleaning supplies without seeing a ghost, pumpkin, or black cat. In December, I don't have to walk through candy canes or Christmas trees to get a loaf of bread.

Walk into any chain store in June and you can't miss it. The Pride display is front and center, impossible to avoid, louder and brighter than Christmas ever gets. Pride flag flying in the front. Meanwhile, Black History Month might earn a poster in the break room if someone remembers.

It feels like a middle finger saying "Fuck you" to the majority of people and especially to the ones that actually keep the lights on. They learned to strip mine a small group of people for profit. A very easily expendable group of people.

I'm not against people celebrating what matters to them. What grates is the performance. The empty gesture dressed up as courage.

Here's how it works: June 1st hits, and the rainbow logo goes live. Mid-month, there's a press release about a donation—usually a number smaller than what they spend on a single Super Bowl ad. By July 1st, the logo's back to normal, the merchandise is clearanced out, and nothing inside the company has actually changed.

The insurance still excludes coverage. The leadership team is still the same. The political donations still flow to candidates who vote against the very rights they claim to champion.

But hey, they changed their Twitter icon for thirty days. That counts, right?

The Gillette Lesson

In 2019, Gillette released an ad called "The Best Men Can Be." It lectured men about toxic masculinity, showed dads pulling their boys away from rough-housing, and basically told half their customer base they were the problem.

The ad went viral, but not the way they hoped. Comments were brutal. Sales dropped. The brand that had spent decades telling men "The Best a Man Can Get" now seemed embarrassed by men entirely.

Within a year, they quietly backed away from the campaign. No apology, no explanation—they just stopped talking about it and hoped everyone would forget.

That's corporate virtue: loud when it's trendy, silent when it costs them.

Nike's Selective Courage

Nike put Colin Kaepernick's face on billboards with the tagline "Believe in something. Even if it means sacrificing everything."

Bold move. Except Nike makes billions manufacturing shoes in countries where workers earn pennies and labor rights barely exist. They'll take a stand on American police brutality but stay quiet about the conditions in their own supply chain.

That's not courage. That's marketing. They calculated that American outrage would generate more buzz than backlash, and they were right. Sales went up. Stock went up. Everyone moved on.

Real sacrifice would be pulling out of factories that exploit workers. But that would actually cost them money, so they stick to the hashtags instead.

The Diversity Industrial Complex

Every Fortune 500 company now has a Chief Diversity Officer. Entire departments dedicated to "equity and inclusion." Mandatory training sessions where you learn which words are acceptable this quarter.

I sat through one of these at the restaurant I managed. Four hours in a conference room, watching PowerPoint slides about microaggressions, unconscious bias, and privilege. The trainer kept apologizing, saying, "I know this feels like overkill, but it's company policy."

At the end, we signed a form saying we completed the training. Nothing changed. Not one thing about how we hired, promoted, or treated people. But the company could check a box and say they were "committed to diversity."

Meanwhile, the actual workforce—the people cooking, serving, cleaning—looked the same as it always had. The only diversity was in the slideshow.

When the Costume Slips

We've seen what happens when brands get tested.

A few years back, Disney stayed silent while Florida passed laws restricting certain classroom discussions about gender and sexuality. Their employees revolted, forcing the company to issue a statement and threaten to pull business from the state.

Except Disney still films in countries where being gay can land you in prison or worse. They edit movies to remove same-sex references for foreign markets. They talk a big game in America because it's safe here. Everywhere else, they fold.

Anheuser-Busch sent a single custom Bud Light can to a trans influencer, and the internet lost its mind. Boycotts spread. Sales tanked. The company panicked, distanced themselves from the partnership, and threw their marketing team under the bus.

There was no conviction there to begin with. Just a test balloon that popped.

Starbucks flies Pride flags and plasters stores with inclusive messaging. But when baristas tried to unionize, the company fought them tooth and nail. Turns out "equity" stops at the payroll department.

The Double Standard at Work

You can avoid the Pride cereal box if you want. Just walk past it.

You can't avoid your employer.

Workplaces now roll out June campaigns like it's a state religion. Rainbow badges appear on internal systems. Meetings open with land acknowledgments. Pronouns go in email signatures—not because you asked, but because it's "encouraged."

Skip the Pride panel? Someone notices.

Decline to add pronouns? You're suddenly "not aligned with company values."

Don't wear the rainbow lanyard? HR might want a word.

Nobody says, "Believe this or you're fired." They don't have to. You feel it in the air, in the performance reviews, in who gets promoted and who gets labeled "difficult."

Meanwhile, you can't say "Merry Christmas" without checking if it's okay. You can't keep a Bible on your desk without someone side-eyeing you. But the Pride flag flies out front for a month and you're expected to cheer.

One belief system gets parades, panels, and corporate backing. The other gets "keep that to yourself."

Not About Hate

Let me be clear: I've worked alongside gay people my whole life. Good people. People I respected. I've seen what it costs someone to finally say, "This is who I am," after years of hiding. I don't wish them harm.

What I resent is being forced to celebrate something I don't believe in to keep my paycheck. Watching companies strip-mine real people's struggles for profit, then toss them aside come July. Seeing kids dragged into adult conversations because some marketing team needed a new angle.

You don't fix discrimination against one group by punishing another. You don't win hearts by holding jobs hostage. And you don't create tolerance by forcing applause.

The Nike Equation

Here's the truth every corporation understands: virtue is profitable until it isn't.

They don't sit in boardrooms debating right and wrong. They debate cost-benefit. If Pride messaging boosts sales, they do it. If it hurts the bottom line, they drop it. The rainbow's just another SKU.

So don't expect them to lead any moral revolution. Their loyalty is to shareholders, not values. The second the wind shifts, they'll shift with it, and the people they claimed to champion will be left holding an empty gesture and a discontinued T-shirt.

Pushing Back Without Screaming

You don't fight this with outrage. You fight it with quiet choices.

Stop buying from brands that treat you like a test market. Reward companies that serve everyone without picking sides. Build skills that make you less dependent on any single employer's approval. Protect your boundaries at work—document everything, know your rights, don't sign what you don't believe.

And stay human. The cashier in the rainbow apron isn't your enemy. They're just trying to get through their shift. Aim your frustration at systems, not the person at the bottom of the food chain.

The Real Revolution

The revolution isn't boycotts or social media wars. It's millions of regular people quietly refusing to play along.

Every time you say, "No thanks, I'll pass on that training," you slow the machine.

Every time you support a local business that doesn't lecture you, you build an alternative.

Every time you raise kids who know the difference between performance and principle, you create the future the corporations can't buy.

One quiet "no" doesn't look like much. But stack enough of them together, and it becomes the only thing they can't ignore—because it's the one thing they can't monetize.

Corporate virtue isn't about values. It's about markets. The second we stop being a profitable audience, they'll move on to the next cause, the next flag, the next thirty-day campaign.

Until then, remember: the rainbow they're selling isn't about pride. It's about profit. And the only color that really matters to them is green.

You and your cause was just a quick buck, before you were put away and pulled back out of the closet next year.

Chapter 15:

The Fairness Crisis
in Modern Sports
Sports Used to Be Simple

There was a time when sports were straightforward. You lined up, you competed, and the best athlete won. You might not have liked the outcome, but you could respect it because everyone was playing by the same rules, in the same category, with the same basic biological equipment.

That's changing now, and nowhere has the shift been more obvious than in women's sports.

The Photo That Broke the Spell

In March 2022, a photo from the NCAA Women's Swimming Championships started circulating online. Two women stood beside the podium: Riley Gaines and Lia Thomas. They had tied for fifth in the 200-yard freestyle. Same time. Same place.

But there was only one fifth-place trophy.

The NCAA handed it to Lia Thomas, a transgender woman who had spent three seasons on the men's team at the University of Pennsylvania before competing on the women's team. Riley was told she'd get a trophy in the mail later.

That image—one athlete holding hardware, the other holding nothing—hit people in a place politics doesn't usually reach. Whatever you think about gender identity, it was hard to shake the feeling that something was off.

You didn't need a PhD in physiology to see the imbalance. You just needed eyes.

What Really Changed

Before transitioning, Lia Thomas competed in men's events with decent but not headline-grabbing results—ranked 462nd in the men's 200 freestyle, 554th in the men's 500 freestyle.

After transitioning and moving into women's competition, those times became dominant. First place finishes. Record-breaking performances. National rankings.

That's the point most people miss. Yes, the times slowed compared to Lia's men's performances. But relative to the women's field, they jumped to the top.

Hormone therapy reduces some advantages, but it doesn't rewind puberty. Male puberty builds a body with a bigger frame, longer limbs, larger lung capacity, greater bone density, and different muscle distribution.

Those advantages don't disappear with testosterone suppression. They're baked into the skeleton, the reach, the capacity.

We all know this without reading a single study. That's why men's sports records are faster, higher, and stronger across virtually every measurable category. That's why women's sports exist as a separate category at all.

If adult male and female bodies were interchangeable for athletic performance, there wouldn't be a need for women's divisions.

It's Not Just Swimming

This isn't an isolated case. We're watching this pattern repeat across multiple sports:

Cycling: In 2019, Rachel McKinnon (now Veronica Ivy) became the first transgender woman to win a world championship track cycling event, beating two biological women to the podium. McKinnon was previously a competitive male cyclist who transitioned in their thirties.

Weightlifting: Laurel Hubbard competed in the Tokyo Olympics in 2021 as the first openly transgender athlete at the Games, having previously competed as a male weightlifter. Hubbard set junior records as a male lifter that stood for years.

Track and Field: CeCé Telfer, who ran on the men's track team at Franklin Pierce University, transitioned and later won an NCAA Division II women's championship in the 400-meter hurdles. As a male athlete, Telfer never placed higher than 200th nationally. As a female athlete, Telfer became a national champion.

Rugby: In New Zealand women's rugby, several trans women have dominated local competitions, leading to injuries among biological female players and protests from teams who felt overmatched physically.

The pattern is unmistakable. Athletes who were middle-of-the-pack or lower in men's competition become champions, record-breakers, and podium finishers in women's competition.

The One-Way Street Problem

Here's the issue almost nobody wants to talk about openly: this is a one-way street.

We now have multiple examples of male-to-female trans athletes entering women's divisions and winning in swimming, weightlifting, cycling, combat sports, and track.

What we don't have are examples of female-to-male trans athletes entering elite men's divisions and dominating.

If identity alone erased the average physical gap between male and female bodies, we'd eventually see a woman transition to male and walk through the UFC heavyweight division. Or crack NFL rosters. Or start winning men's Olympic events.

We haven't. And we won't.

Because this isn't about identity. It's about bodies.

The average biological male has about 40% more upper body strength than the average biological female. Men have larger hearts, greater lung capacity, denser bones, and a higher percentage of fast-twitch muscle fiber.

Testosterone suppression reduces some of these advantages, but it doesn't eliminate them. Studies show that even after years of hormone therapy, trans women retain significant advantages in strength, speed, and power compared to biological women.

This isn't bigotry. It's biology. And pretending otherwise doesn't protect anyone—it just hurts the women who've spent their lives training to compete fairly.

When Fairness Became Bigotry

The common refrain is: "Trans women are women. Full stop. Excluding them from women's sports is discrimination."

But that framing leaves out half the people involved—the biological women themselves.

Women's sports exist for a reason: to give biological females a dedicated space to compete fairly with each other. We separated sports by sex for the same reason we separate them by weight class in boxing and wrestling—because physical differences matter, and fair competition requires accounting for them.

When someone who went through male puberty—with the bone structure, muscle mass, height, reach, and lung capacity that comes with it—steps into a women's category, you're not just including one person.

You're changing the field for everyone else in it.

You're asking women and girls to give up records, podiums, scholarships, and opportunities so that one person's identity can be fully affirmed in every possible space.

That's not inclusion. That's erasure of boundaries in service of ideology.

The Locker Room
Nobody Talks About

There's another part of this that gets whispered about but rarely said out loud: the locker rooms.

Riley Gaines has spoken publicly about sharing a locker room with Lia Thomas at the NCAA championships. About standing there, trying to change, feeling uncomfortable, and being told that voicing that discomfort made her a bigot.

Female athletes across multiple sports have quietly expressed similar concerns. They don't want to be seen as intolerant, so they stay silent. But the discomfort is real.

We spent decades fighting for women to have their own spaces, their own facilities, their own safe places to compete and prepare. Now we're being told those boundaries are discriminatory, and any woman who objects is the problem.

That's not progress. That's gaslighting.

The Trust Problem

Sports used to be the one place where you could still believe what you saw. The ball went through the hoop or it didn't. The time on the clock was faster or it wasn't. The lift was heavier or it wasn't.

Now, people are being told: "Don't trust your eyes. Don't trust your gut. Trust the policy. Trust the experts. Trust that this is fair even when everything you see tells you it isn't."

If you say, "This doesn't seem fair," you're labeled hateful, transphobic, a bigot.

If you ask questions, you're told to educate yourself, do better, check your privilege.

Meanwhile, the same institutions that botched trust during COVID, that told us masks didn't work and then did work, that changed guidelines every other week—now say, "Trust us on this too."

You can't have it both ways. You can't treat female athletes as expendable political props, ignore their concerns, silence their objections, and then act shocked when people stop believing in the integrity of the whole system.

What About the Kids?

This isn't just happening at the elite level. It's filtering down to high school sports. Middle school sports. Youth leagues.

A biological male who identifies as female can now compete against girls who've trained their whole lives, girls who are smaller, weaker, slower by no fault of their own—just by virtue of being female.

And those girls are learning a brutal lesson: your effort doesn't matter as much as someone else's biology.

My granddaughters are in sports. They work hard. They practice. They push themselves. And I'll be damned if I'm going to tell them that all that work doesn't matter because fairness got sacrificed on the altar of inclusivity.

They deserve to compete against other girls. Not against biological males who have every physical advantage nature can provide.

A Simple, Honest Solution

The answer isn't complicated. Keep women's sports for biological women.

Create open or additional categories if there are enough trans athletes who want to compete. We already use categories in sports—weight classes, age brackets, disability classifications.

We don't call those hateful. We call them fair.

If we truly care about inclusion, we should build fair ways for everyone to compete. If we truly care about fairness, we must protect the one thing women have fought for decades to build: a level playing field against other women.

This isn't about denying anyone's identity. It's about preserving fair competition. Those two things aren't the same, and pretending they are doesn't help anyone.

The Studies Game

You'll hear people say, "Studies show there's no advantage after hormone therapy."

You'll hear other people say, "Studies show the advantage remains."

Here's the truth: you can find a study to support almost any position you want. Research is expensive. It gets funded by people with agendas. Results get interpreted through ideological lenses.

Search engines are designed by people with beliefs, but mostly their wallets. They are easily built to push you to whoever's paying. Its part of the controlling of sheep. It's how you receive the information they want you to or "The truth" you take in and then spit out to everyone you can. So, the studies can be whatever outcome they want, and the search engines can send you to whatever they want.

But I don't need a study to tell me what I can see with my own eyes.

I see who's standing on the podium. I see who's breaking records. I see which direction the talent flows.

And so do you.

What Happens If We Don't Fix This

If we don't address this now, here's what's coming:

Women's sports records will increasingly be held by biological males

Scholarships will go to athletes with insurmountable physical advantages

Girls will quit sports because they know they can't win

The category of "women's sports" will become meaningless

And then what? Do we go back and strip medals? Do we rewrite record books? Do we admit we made a mistake and apologize to all the girls who lost opportunities?

Or do we just shrug and say, "Well, that's progress"?

The worst part is we're taking athletes—people we're supposed to celebrate and admire—and turning them into political pawns. We're dragging them into culture war mud when all they wanted to do was compete.

That's not fair to the trans athletes. And it's sure as hell not fair to the women.

The Closing Beat

Separate the categories. Biology vs. biology. Trans vs. trans. Open divisions for those who don't fit the traditional categories.

That way, when someone wins, everyone knows it was fair. The competition was legitimate. The victory was earned.

Protecting women's sports isn't discrimination. It's defending the reality that biology matters, that fairness matters, and that women deserve their own space to compete against other women.

My granddaughters deserve to race other girls.

Not to be told they're bigots for noticing when the playing field isn't level.

Not to be told that fairness is less important than feelings.

Not to lose before they even start because someone decided biology doesn't matter.

That's not the world I want to leave them.

And if you've got daughters, granddaughters, nieces, or any girls you care about, it shouldn't be the world you want either.

Chapter 16:

Men, You Are Not Defective
The Lie You've Been Told

If you're in your late teens, twenties, maybe thirties, you've grown up hearing one message over and over:

"There's something wrong with you."

Your energy? Problem.

Your competitiveness? Toxic.

Your desire to lead, build, protect? Probably patriarchal.

From grade school on, you were told to sit still in classrooms built for quiet, docile kids. If you couldn't, they talked about medicating you. Ritalin, Adderall, whatever it took to make you manageable.

You were told to "use your words" when what you needed was to run, to climb, to wrestle, to do something with your hands and your body that burned off the restless energy coursing through you.

Then you hit the workplace, and the message didn't change. It just got more sophisticated:

"Step back and make space."

"Check your privilege."

"Don't be so aggressive."

"Read the room."

You've been told, more or less, that your natural wiring—the very thing that makes you male—is dangerous, outdated, problematic.

I'm here to tell you: it isn't. You're not defective for being a man.

The Day I Realized
They Were Wrong

I was working at the environment clean up company, when I watched something that stuck with me.

A new guy—college educated, bright kid, said all the right things in the interview—showed up for his first week. Second day on the job, we had an equipment failure. Motor overheated, smoke everywhere, alarms going off.

The foreman looked at the new guy and said, "Help me pull this motor out before it catches."

The kid froze. Just stood there, staring, while three of us moved. Not because he was scared—because he'd never in his life been in a situation where hesitation could cost you.

He'd been raised to think, to analyze, to consider all options before acting.

After we got it handled, the foreman pulled him aside. Not mean, just clear: "Out here, thinking is good. But sometimes you just have to do. You'll learn."

The kid did learn. Turned out to be solid once he understood the rhythm. But I never forgot that moment.

Because that's what we're doing to an entire generation of boys. We're training them to hesitate, to second-guess, to wait for permission. And then we're shocked when they can't act decisively when it matters.

What Masculinity Is Actually For

Masculinity isn't the problem. What you do with it is what matters.

The same traits that can make a man dangerous when twisted—strength, aggression, stubbornness, competitiveness—are the exact traits that run into burning buildings, stand between danger and a family, build businesses from nothing, and keep countries from collapsing.

The same culture that tells you "Men are the problem" is the first one to dial 911 when something goes wrong.

When Hurricane Harvey hit Houston in 2017, who do you think showed up with boats? Who waded into chest-deep water pulling people off roofs? Who worked eighteen-hour shifts at the plant to keep the power on?

It wasn't a committee. It wasn't a focus group. It was men—most of them the exact kind of "toxic masculine" men the internet loves to mock—doing what needed to be done because nobody else was going to do it.

When the power goes out, when the pipes burst, when the truck breaks down on the highway, when danger shows up at the door—nobody's asking about your pronouns or your feelings about traditional gender roles.

They're asking: Can you fix this? Can you handle this? Can you stand between this problem and the people who need protection?

That's not sexism. That's reality.

The Classroom Tried to Break You

Let me tell you something about the education system: it wasn't built for boys.

Sit still for six hours. Don't fidget. Don't tap your pencil. Don't get out of your seat. Listen to lectures. Take notes. Regurgitate information on tests.

For girls, who tend to develop verbal skills and fine motor control earlier, who are generally better at sitting still and following sequential instructions—that system works fine.

For boys? It's torture.

Boys are wired for movement, for hands-on learning, for competition, for tangible results. You tell a boy to sit still and listen for an hour; you're fighting against thousands of years of evolutionary biology.

But instead of adapting the system to how boys actually learn, we decided boys were broken.

So, we started medicating them. Roughly 70% of ADHD diagnoses are boys. Not because boys are defective. Because we built a system that treats normal male energy as a disorder.

You weren't broken. The system was. And it tried to convince you otherwise.

The Pressure to Apologize for Existing

Young men today twist themselves into knots trying to be "good allies," trying to prove they're "not like other guys," trying to apologize for traits they can't help having.

They post about how they're "learning" and "doing better" and "checking their privilege" like they're in some kind of perpetual penance for being born male.

Here's what I want you to understand: you don't need to apologize for being strong. For wanting to protect people you love. For wanting to win. For wanting to build something that lasts.

You don't need to apologize for taking up space in the world.

But here's what you do need to do: channel those traits productively.

What to Do with the Fire

That aggression you feel? That competitive drive? That restless energy? Don't suppress it. Direct it.

Channel it into your body:

Lift heavy things. Learn to fight—properly, with discipline and respect. Box. Wrestle. Train jiu-jitsu. Not to hurt people, but to understand what your body can do, to learn control, to earn the confidence that comes from knowing you could handle yourself if you had to.

Channel it into creation:

Build something. Fix engines. Work with wood. Learn a trade. There's something primal and satisfying about making something with your hands, about seeing tangible results from your effort.

Channel it into protection:

Stand up for someone smaller getting pushed around. Be the guy people can rely on when things go wrong. Be steady when everyone else is panicking.

Channel it into excellence:

Outwork people. Be so good at what you do that they can't ignore you. Create instead of consume. Become the kind of man others want on their team when it matters.

The fire inside you is not the problem. Letting it burn without direction is the problem.

The Men We the World Needs

We don't need men who are softer, more compliant, more agreeable.

We need men who can stand on their own two feet.

Who keep their word.

Who show up on time.

Who do the job right even when nobody's watching.

Who tell the truth even when it costs them.

We need dads who discipline and love their kids.

Husbands who protect and honor their wives.

Brothers and friends who push each other to be better, not weaker.

We need men who understand that strength isn't about dominating others—it's about having the capacity to help, protect, and build, and choosing to do so.

The Iron Law

There's an iron law the culture doesn't want you to know: when things really fall apart, they call for men.

Not the sensitivity-trained, perpetually apologizing, "I'm still learning" men.

They call for the men who can fix the furnace at 2 AM. Who can change the tire in the rain. Who can pull people out of flood water. Who can stand between danger and the vulnerable. Who can make the hard call when everyone else is frozen.

Those are the men who keep civilization running. And they're getting rarer.

Because we've spent thirty years telling boys that those traits are toxic, that needing to be strong is insecure, that wanting to protect is controlling.

The Sneering at Masculinity

When someone sneers at "traditional masculinity," you know what they're really sneering at?

The men who:

Showed up at 6 AM to rebuild their neighbor's fence after the storm

Taught their sons to change a tire and look a man in the eye

Worked overtime to keep food on the table

Fixed things instead of replacing them

Said "I'll handle it" and then handled it

They're sneering at the men who built everything they take for granted.

The bridges they drive over. The buildings they work in. The power lines that keep their laptops charged. The plumbing that brings water to their tap.

All of it—built, maintained, and repaired by men doing the kind of work that gets mocked as "toxic masculinity" on Twitter.

The Closing Beat

Here's what I want you to remember:

You are not a walking problem to be solved.

You are not defective for being a man.

You are raw material—and what you build with it is up to you.

The world is going to keep telling you to sit down, be quiet, make yourself smaller, apologize for taking up space.

Don't.

Be strong, but use that strength to lift others.

Be aggressive, but aim it at problems, not people.

Be competitive, but compete against your own limits.

Be stubborn, but about things that matter.

When the pipe bursts, when the power goes out, when the storm hits, when danger shows up—they're going to call you.

And you'll be glad you didn't listen when they told you to become something lesser.

The men who built the world you inherited didn't ask permission. They didn't apologize for being capable. They didn't wait for approval.

They just did the work.

Be that kind of man.

The world needs you more than it's willing to admit.

Chapter 17:

The Porch in Your Pocket
The Day the Porch Came Home

I remember the exact moment my phone stopped being a tool and started being a porch. It was a hot afternoon, and I was waiting for the AC repairman. The house was already sweltering, and the fan was just pushing hot air around. I grabbed my phone to check the time, and that's when it happened.

I opened Twitter—just to kill a few minutes. A notification popped up: some stranger had replied to a comment I'd made days ago. Nothing important, just a snarky remark about a news story. But the reply was pure venom. I felt my pulse spike. My fingers tightened around the phone. I started typing a response, my thumbs moving faster than my brain. I was mad before I even knew why.

That's when it hit me: I wasn't just on the porch. I was carrying it. Everywhere.

The Gossip's New Home

Every small town used to have a gossip. You knew where she lived. You knew that if you walked past her porch, she'd be watching. She knew who was pregnant, whose truck was parked where it shouldn't be, who had left the bar with whose husband. If you wanted peace, you stayed away from that porch.

But now? The porch is in your pocket. It's always there, always watching, always whispering. And unlike the old gossip, this one doesn't just talk to the neighbors—it talks to the whole world.

The Algorithm That Feeds the Fire

Scrolling used to feel harmless. A few funny clips. A couple of news stories. A picture of someone's dinner. But the scroll changed. It learned. It studied what makes us stare, pause, and rage.

People think the apps are free. They're wrong. You pay with your attention. You pay with your peace. Your anger is the product.

Open your feed now and see what jumps out: the craziest liberal in Portland, the wildest conservative in Florida, the most extreme teacher, cop, protester. All edited, clipped, and captioned to make you mad. You're not seeing your neighbor mowing his lawn or the kid bagging groceries to help at home. You're seeing the handful of people in a country of 330 million who will most reliably make you angry.

Every swipe is a pull on a slot machine rigged for outrage. Maybe you hit something that feels good. Maybe you hit something that makes you mad. Either way, you keep going.

The apps love anger. Anger keeps you hooked. Happy people don't comment much. Angry people comment all day. The algorithm whispers: "See? That's what they're like." Whoever you already suspect is ruining the country becomes the caricature you're fed. The more you believe it, the longer you stay. The longer you stay, the more ads they sell.

It's a silent war over your attention, and the angrier you are, the richer they get.

The Lie We Tell Ourself on the Porch

Most of us say the same lie: "I can stop anytime. I'm just observing the gossip."

If that were true, the phone wouldn't be the last thing we see before bed and the first thing we check when we wake up. We sleep with it next to our head like it's a newborn. We use it in bathrooms, parking lots, elevators, at stoplights, during TV shows we say we're watching, while we eat, while we walk, while we talk to real people.

We tell the lie because the truth feels heavier. The truth is simple: We're hooked. We've built a chair on that carried porch, and we can't seem to get up.

Ask someone to sit in a chair with no phone for ten minutes. They'll twitch. They'll reach for it even when they know they don't need it.

Phones made boredom vanish. But boredom wasn't the enemy. Boredom was a break, a walk away from the gossip's gaze. Without breaks, your mind feels like a dryer running on high heat all day. It never stops spinning. It never cools.

The lie keeps us from admitting what the porch really did. It didn't just show us the noise. It convinced us the noise was the whole world.

The Guy in the Dairy Aisle
(A Crack in the Screen)

Not long ago, I was at the grocery store. I'd been scrolling on my phone before I left, and I rounded a corner and saw a man wearing a shirt for a politician I can't stand. My first thought, my phone-trained reflex, was: "Look at this idiot. He's what's wrong with America."

Right then, he dropped his keys. Before I could even think about it, I bent down, picked them up, and handed them to him. "Here you go, man."

He smiled. "Thanks, partner." That was it.

In that split second, the screen cracked. The algorithm in my pocket wanted me to see him as an enemy. Real life told me he was just a neighbor. The shirt was real, but so was the smile. So were his car keys. So was the fact that he was buying milk and bread and probably hated his bills, traffic, and gas prices just as much as I did.

This is the rage we carry without knowing. The phone trains your brain to react before you think. It rewards quick anger and punishes patience. You start expecting drama everywhere. You forget what calm feels like. There's a tone people use on the porch that they'd never use face-to-face, typing like they're swinging an axe.

When you live there too much, that tone leaks into your real life. You snap faster. You judge quicker.

The real world is calmer than the online world. But when you live on your phone, you bring it with you everywhere. The Guy in the Dairy Aisle was a reminder: he didn't need to be converted or canceled. He just needed his keys.

The Fake Fame
of the
Porch Show

Another part of the trap is the false idea that we're all public figures now. The porch convinces us everyone has a stage. At first, that sounded great.

Then it changed how we live.

People now stage their lives like a TV show for the porch audience. They pose meals. They pose moments. They pose kids. Everything becomes content. A good day doesn't count until the porch sees it. A bad day doesn't count unless strangers weigh in.

The worst part is the constant, carried judgment. You post something simple. Someone finds a reason to twist it. Someone calls you a name. Someone takes a shot. And it sticks with you. You carry strangers' opinions like heavy bags you never meant to pick up.

Humans weren't meant to have thousands of tiny voices shaping their self-worth from a pocket-sized porch. We weren't made to measure our value in likes. We weren't made to perform for an algorithm. The fame the porch offers is fake. The damage it does to our sense of self is real.

The Night I Caught Myself
Doom-Scrolling

I was sitting on the couch, scrolling through my phone, my thumb moving faster than my brain could process. I was angry—about what, I couldn't even say. My wife walked in and asked, "What are you doing?"

I looked up, dazed. "Nothing."

"Then why do you look like you're about to punch a wall?"

I didn't have an answer. I was just scrolling, feeding the machine, letting it feed me back anger and frustration. I put the phone down and realized: I wasn't avoiding boredom. I was avoiding thinking. Avoiding the quiet. Avoiding the fact that I was tired, that I was worried about my kid's grades, that I was frustrated with work. The porch was easier than facing any of that.

Putting the Porch Down

Phones aren't going away. And we don't need them to. We're not throwing the porch in a lake. But we must learn to put it down.

Here's the truth they don't want you to know on the porch: Your attention is a vote. Every time you click the crazy headline, watch the "Can you believe this?" video, or share the most extreme example, you're voting. You're telling the machine: "More of this, please."

And it delivers.

We must set rules that give us our lives back. Simple rules like:

Do not bring the porch to bed.

Do not let it be your last sight at night or your first in the morning.

Do not bring the porch to meals. Eat with people, or with your own thoughts.

Do not bring the porch when you're angry or bored.

Do not feed the fire or seek a distraction from it.

Do something real for every hour on the porch. Fix something. Build something. Cook something. Call someone.

Do not argue with strangers on the porch. They don't know you, and you won't change them there.

Most importantly: when you feel the hate rising at "those people," ask yourself: "Have I actually met anyone like this in my real life?" If the answer is no, the problem isn't your neighbor. It's the app.

What You Find
When You Walk Away

When you put the porch down, even a little, something surprising happens.

You start to feel grounded. Your mind slows. The world looks calmer. You remember how to focus. You get time back. Time to think. Time to rest. Time to live.

The phone gave us everything fast. It never gave us space. Space is where life happens. You begin to see people as people again, not caricatures or enemies. You hear tone. You see eyes. You learn things no screen can show. You reconnect with the reality that most people will hold the door, say "thanks" if you let them merge, and apologize if they bump into you.

The constant, low-grade irritation lifts. The dryer in your mind finally stops spinning. You remember what silence feels like. And silence is what the porch fears most, because silence gives you back the control you handed over.

The Truth We Must Speak from the Ground

The phone isn't evil. But the porch it builds is powerful. Powerful enough to shape our moods, our habits, our relationships, and even our beliefs.

It can be a tool. Or it can be a porch you never leave, where you see the world only through the warped lens of gossip and outrage.

Most people never get brave enough to admit they live there. But admission is the first real step off of it.

You don't have to be perfect. You just have to be aware. Awareness is what cuts the strings. Awareness is what lets you choose the real aisle over the virtual porch.

The hate machine only works when you carry its porch everywhere and believe its view is the only view.

Turn it down.

Slow it.

Control it.

Make it small again.

Your life is bigger than a screen. Your peace is worth more than a scroll. Your real, messy, human connections are more vital than any virtual feud.

This chapter ends with one simple truth: You were not built to live on a porch of outrage, carried in your pocket. But you were built to step off it, onto solid ground. And you can start that journey today. Just put it down, and look up. The real world, calmer, kinder, and more complex than you've been told, is waiting for you.

And if you're wondering where to start? Remember the chicken lady from Chapter 1—the one in the Burger King crown, screaming about kings in a Beaumont parking lot? She's still out there, still angry, still performing for the porch. But you don't have to join her. You can walk away. You can choose real life instead.

So put the porch down. Step off. And come back to the world that's waiting for you.

Chapter 18:

What We Lost

We didn't lose these things in one loud crash. We lost them quietly, piece by piece, until one day we woke up and realized the scaffolding that held us together was gone. Privacy, belonging, forgiveness, excitement—none of them were luxuries. They were the bones of a life that made sense. Strip them away, and you don't just get a different culture. You get weaker people.

Privacy:
The Freedom to Outgrow Yourself

There was a time when mistakes died in the moment. You mouthed off, you got punished, and the story ended with the people who saw it. No screenshots. No permanent record. No digital scarlet letter that followed you into adulthood. You could grow up, move three streets over, and reinvent yourself. Privacy wasn't a luxury—it was oxygen. It gave you room to breathe, to stumble, to recover, and to try again without the whole world watching.

I remember being fifteen, skipping school. I must have been seen somewhere. By the time I got home, my mom already knew. That was the price of living in a nosy town. But here's the difference: the punishment was local. It was contained. My reputation wasn't blasted across a feed or archived in some permanent file. I served my sentence, learned my lesson, and walked away with a clean slate. That's what privacy gave us—the chance to grow past our worst day.

Today, that slate doesn't exist. Every dumb thing is recorded, searchable, and weaponized. A teenager posts a joke, and ten years later it's dragged out in a job interview. A kid loses his temper, and the video circulates before the fight is even over. We've built a culture where mistakes are permanent, and forgiveness is optional. Privacy used to be the buffer between who you were and who you could become. Strip it away, and you don't just lose secrets—you lose the freedom to change.

Think about the difference between a diary and a timeline. A diary is private. You write your thoughts, your fears, your mistakes, and you close the book. Maybe you burn it later. A timeline is public. Every thought is broadcast, every mistake is archived, every bad take is screenshot by someone who doesn't even like you. A diary lets you grow. A timeline traps you in amber.

The irony is that we gave privacy away willingly. We traded it for convenience, for likes, for the dopamine hit of being seen. We installed cameras on our porches, microphones in our kitchens, trackers in our pockets. We told ourselves it was progress. But progress without privacy is surveillance. And surveillance doesn't just watch—it judges. It freezes you in place. It makes reinvention impossible.

I've seen grown men lose jobs over a joke from college. I've seen teenagers branded for life over a video taken in anger. And I've seen people stop speaking honestly because they know the record is permanent. That's the real loss. Privacy didn't just protect your secrets—it protected your courage. It gave you the freedom to say something dumb, to test an idea, to risk being wrong. Without it, people don't grow. They perform. They curate. They hide.

Back in Port Neches, privacy wasn't about hiding—it was about living. You could screw up, pay for it, and move on. You could reinvent yourself after graduation. You could leave behind the worst version of yourself and step into something better. That's gone now. Today, your worst version is the one the world remembers. And the world never forgets.

Here's the sting: without privacy, you don't just lose secrets—you lose the chance to grow. And a culture that refuses to let people grow is a culture that collapses under the weight of its own judgment.

Belonging:
From Neighbors to Numbers

Belonging used to be simple. It wasn't something you had to define, measure, or post about. It was Friday night football at The Reservation, where the whole town squeezed onto the bleachers and you felt like part of something bigger. It was looping Central Mall on a Saturday night, checking who was holding hands by the fountain, who just got dumped by the pretzel stand, and who was brave enough to ask someone out in person. It was riding bikes until the streetlights buzzed on, knowing you'd find your friends by spotting a pile of bikes in somebody's yard. Belonging wasn't abstract—it was physical. You could see it, hear it, and feel it.

In Port Neches, belonging meant your neighbors knew your name, your teachers knew your parents, and your teammates knew whether you'd show up to practice. It wasn't always comfortable. Sometimes it felt nosy, even suffocating. But it was real. You didn't have to wonder if you mattered—you did, because people noticed when you weren't there. That's the kind of belonging that keeps kids from drifting too far, that catches you when you fall, that reminds you you're part of a net.

Today, belonging has been outsourced to algorithms. It's measured in followers, likes, and engagement rates. Instead of neighbors, we have numbers. Instead of teammates, we have timelines. Instead of showing up, we log in. And the cruel trick is that it looks like connection. You can have thousands of followers and still be alone. You can be "seen" by strangers across the world and still have nobody to call when your truck breaks down. We traded community for crowds, and the result is loneliness dressed up as popularity.

I've watched grown men chase belonging online like teenagers chasing approval in a mall food court. They post, they refresh, they count. And when the numbers don't add up, they feel invisible. But here's the truth: belonging isn't about being seen—it's about being known. Your neighbor borrowing your ladder knows you. Your buddy showing up at the drag strip knows you. A stranger clicking "like" on a post doesn't. That's the difference between community and crowd. One anchors you. The other leaves you drifting.

The irony is that people know something's missing. You can hear it in the way they talk about "finding their tribe" or "building community." But instead of walking across the street, they join another online group. Instead of knocking on a neighbor's door, they start another Discord server. The hunger is real, but the solution is fake. Belonging doesn't happen in curated spaces—it happens in messy ones. It happens when you're stuck mowing the yard with your dad, when you're sweating through practice with teammates, when you're sitting in church pews next to people you don't even like but still respect. That's the grit of real belonging. It's not always fun, but it's always grounding.

I think about the kids growing up now, their belonging measured in streaks on Snapchat or likes on TikTok. What happens when those streaks break? What happens when the likes stop? They crumble, because their belonging was never real to begin with. It was conditional, fragile, and temporary. And when belonging is fragile, people are fragile too.

Here's the sting: we traded neighbors for numbers, and the math never adds up. Belonging isn't about how many people see you—it's about who shows up when you need them. And until we remember that, we'll keep mistaking crowds for community and wondering why we still feel alone.

Forgiveness:
The Muscle We Forgot to Use

Forgiveness used to be a survival skill. It wasn't optional—it was how you kept moving. You screwed up, you apologized, and people let you move on. It didn't erase the mistake, but it gave you a future. Without forgiveness, every scar would have been a sentence. With it, scars became lessons.

I remember the soap punishment in our house. One slip of the tongue, one F-bomb dropped in front of my little brother, and my mom was on me like a sniper. Ivory bar across the tongue, bubbles in my mouth, shame in my eyes. It was brutal, but here's the thing: when it was over, it was over. I rinsed, I apologized, and life went on. My mom didn't drag it out for weeks. She didn't remind me of it every time I opened my mouth. She forgave me, and that forgiveness gave me room to grow.

Same with fights. You squared up behind the gym, threw a couple of swings, maybe caught a bloody nose, and when it was done, it was done. A handshake, a nod, or just silence—but it was closure. You weren't branded forever as "the kid who fought." You were the kid who learned. Forgiveness was baked into the rhythm of life. It wasn't soft. It wasn't sentimental. It was practical. Without it, the whole system would have collapsed under grudges.

Today, forgiveness is treated like weakness. One wrong word, one bad joke, one misstep—and you're branded forever. Screenshots, viral posts, permanent records. People don't forgive because they don't have to. They can punish instead. They can cancel. They can archive your worst moment and replay it until you're crushed under the weight of it. Forgiveness has been replaced by judgment, and judgment has no expiration date.

The irony is that forgiveness was never about excusing bad behavior. It was about giving people a chance to change. My dad used to say, "You don't raise kids to be perfect. You raise them to be better tomorrow than they were today." That only works if tomorrow is possible. If every mistake is permanent, tomorrow never comes. You're stuck in the worst version of yourself, with no way out.

I've seen what happens when forgiveness disappears. People stop taking risks. They stop speaking honestly. They stop trying. Why? Because the cost of failure is too high. If you can't be forgiven, you can't afford to fail. And if you can't afford to fail, you can't grow. Forgiveness was the muscle that let us lift ourselves out of mistakes. Without it, people stay weak.

Think about the difference between a scar and a wound. A scar means you healed. A wound means you're still bleeding. Forgiveness is what turns wounds into scars. It's what lets people carry their past without being crushed by it. Without forgiveness, we're all just bleeding endlessly, waiting for someone to point at the stain.

Here's the sting: without forgiveness, every scar becomes a sentence. And a culture that refuses to forgive is a culture that eats itself alive. We didn't just lose kindness—we lost the muscle that makes growth possible. And until we remember how to use it, we'll keep raising people who crumble under the weight of their own mistakes.

Excitement:
The Thrill That Needed Waiting

Excitement used to be earned. It wasn't something you could order up with a click or stream instantly on demand. It was built slowly, like pressure in a pipe, until the release was worth the wait. Friday night football, saving for a concert ticket, standing in line for a movie you'd been hearing about for months—that anticipation was half the thrill. The waiting sharpened the edge. The payoff felt alive because you had to endure the stretch before it arrived.

I remember sitting in a tire shop as a kid, bored out of my skull while my dad waited for a rotation. No phone, no tablet, no endless scroll to kill the time. Just me, a stack of outdated magazines, and the smell of rubber. At the time, it felt like torture. But boredom had a strange way of turning into excitement. By the time we left, even something as simple as stopping for a snow cone felt like a victory. The boredom made the small reward feel bigger. That's the math of anticipation: the longer you wait, the sweeter the payoff.

Today, excitement has been flattened. Everything is instant. Movies drop on streaming the same day they hit theaters. Music is uploaded at midnight and consumed by breakfast. Games, shows, concerts—nothing requires patience anymore. And when nothing requires patience, excitement loses its teeth. It becomes noise. A constant hum of stimulation that never peaks, never dips, never gives you the rush of waiting and the joy of release.

The irony is that people think they're happier this way. They think instant access means more satisfaction. But ask anyone who grew up waiting for Friday night lights, or saving allowance for a cassette, or standing in line for a blockbuster, and they'll tell you: the waiting was the point. The anticipation gave the event weight. It made it matter. Without waiting, everything feels disposable. You consume it, forget it, and move on to the next thing without ever feeling the thrill.

I've seen kids today scroll through entire seasons of shows in a weekend, then shrug like it was nothing. Compare that to the way we used to wait a whole week for the next episode, talking about it at school, guessing what would happen, building the suspense together. That week of waiting made the payoff communal. It made excitement something you shared. Now it's solitary, silent, and forgettable.

Excitement without waiting is just noise. It's stimulation without meaning. And stimulation without meaning leaves people restless, chasing the next hit, never satisfied. We didn't just lose excitement—we lost the patience that made excitement possible. We lost the buildup, the suspense, the ache that made the release worth it.

Here's the truth: when you erase waiting, you erase wonder. And a culture that refuses to wait is a culture that forgets how to feel joy. Excitement isn't about having everything now—it's about savoring the moment when it finally arrives. Without that, life becomes a blur of instant gratification, and the thrill that once made us feel alive fades into static.

Closing Beat

Privacy, belonging, forgiveness, excitement—none of them were luxuries. They were the bones of a life that made sense. Strip them away, and you don't just get a different culture. You get weaker people.

What we lost wasn't small. It was the scaffolding that held us up. And if we don't rebuild it, the collapse won't be loud—it'll be quiet, steady, and final.

I am glad that everything I did when I was in school is just a rumor. There is no video or podcast, or Facebook feeds of anything I did. My word against maybe one or two other people, if they can even remember it. Not like it is today.

Chapter 19:

The Quiet Revolution
Where the Way Back Starts

I've spent a lot of pages talking about what broke: common sense replaced by policy, reality replaced by performance, institutions selling trust to the highest bidder, screens replacing community, outrage replacing thought.

If the story ends there, this book becomes one long rant. I'm not interested in that.

Because for every sign the world is falling apart, I've seen simple moments that tell a different story. Moments that don't get filmed. Moments that don't trend.

The way back isn't loud. It isn't online. It doesn't come with applause.

It starts in the quiet places—on playgrounds, in garages, on fishing docks, around dinner tables. In the space between "you got this" and "I'm right here."

That's where the real revolution lives.

Tugboat Island

I took one of my kids and a granddaughter to Tugboat Island recently. It's one of those playgrounds designed so no lawyer ever breaks a sweat. Soft turf. Rounded corners. Safety warnings that read like legal disclaimers.

She saw the climbing tower and charged it like it owed her money. Halfway up, her grip slipped. Her feet scraped plastic. For a breath or two, gravity had her.

Every modern parenting instinct screamed: Run. Help. Catch her. Stop the fall.

But she looked back for just a second, eyes fierce, then reached up. Stronger than before. Knuckles white. A stubborn little grunt.

She made it.

When she stood on top, she spun around and yelled: "Paw-Paw! Did you see that?"

I saw it. But more important, she saw what she could do.

No audience. No camera. No like button. Just pride earned by effort.

Real confidence comes from climbing, not scrolling.

The Other Kid

Right then, another boy started up the wall. Same age. Same struggle.

His mom sprinted like she was diving into an action movie. "No! You'll fall!" She hauled him down like she'd saved him from a burning building.

He was fine. His pride wasn't.

He wasn't crying because he was hurt. He was crying because he wasn't allowed to try.

Then she handed him a phone. Instant calm. Blue glow on his face. The playground, wide open behind him, didn't matter anymore.

He learned: I can't do hard things. The world is too dangerous. This screen fixes my feelings.

That's a brutal lesson to teach a child.

In twenty years, he might be great at scrolling. But he may never climb his own mountain.

Magnet Fishing

Another day, one of my grandsons brought me a tablet. "Paw-Paw, look at this! We should try it!"

Some guy on YouTube was magnet fishing—finding coins, bikes, even a safe full of cash. Millions of views.

We could have watched the next video. Instead, I said: "Let's go."

We bought a magnet, rope, gloves. Drove to the canal. He talked the whole way about pirate treasure waiting for us.

Hours passed. No treasure chest of money, just rusty nails, bottle caps, a tangled bike wheel, something that looked like an alien fossil but was probably a muffler. The thing is he was excited like it was treasure.

Then, after a long battle, he dragged up the prize: a waterlogged, grime filled, sludge covered vacuum cleaner. You actually smelled it from 30 feet away.

He screamed like he'd discovered gold. We stared at this dripping, mud-filled eyesore.

"That's not riding in my truck," I said.

He sighed. Thought about it. Nodded. "One man's trash is another man's treasure." I finally talked him out of keeping it. He took a picture, but most of all he made a memory.

We left the vacuum for the trash crew, and he kept fishing. Laughing. Trying. Hopeful.

On the ride home, he didn't ask for the tablet. He asked when we could go again.

He learned: Most adventures don't go viral. Work is fun even when you fail. The story is the reward.

Phones give gratification. Real life gives growth.

Raising Resilient Kids
in a
Fragile World

My grandkids are all different. Ones in jiu-jitsu, ranking her belts. Two are in dance, correcting every mistake. One reads books like oxygen. Another gets knocked down in football. Another runs track until he's gasping.

They complain, argue, slam doors. They are not perfect.

But they do not collapse.

They're learning: hard doesn't mean impossible. Failure isn't final.

We can't control what schools teach or what phones show. But we can control what happens in our homes, in our yards, in our trucks on the way to the canal.

That's where character forms. Not in sanitized classrooms. Not in curated feeds.

The Quiet Revolution

People think saving the country means big speeches and protests. Maybe.

But maybe it looks like this instead: parents calmly asking schools what they're teaching. People choosing skills and trades over chasing clout. Small business owners serving anyone who walks through the door. Kids playing outside until dark instead of doom-scrolling. Families saying grace instead of going viral.

This isn't a loud movement. It's steady. Grounded. Stubborn as hell.

The world wants you frantic and outraged, because frantic people are easy to control.

The most dangerous thing you can be today? Calm.

Your Part

Not everyone needs a platform. Not everyone needs a megaphone.

You can change the world by letting the kid climb. Teaching consequences with love. Fixing something instead of watching others live. Refusing to lie, even when lying is easier. Supporting real people doing real work. Showing up when it matters, not when it trends.

The world may get crazier. You don't have to join it.

You can be the one who says "Try again." The one who steps in when needed. The one who laughs at the madness but doesn't inhale it.

Revolutions don't need forklifts. They need ordinary courage.

The Spark

Change won't start with a bill or a ban.

It starts with moments like this:

A child hangs from a plastic climbing wall. Her grip slips. Her legs shake. She doesn't quit. She reaches. She climbs. She conquers.

She turns to the people who love her and yells: "Did you see that?"

We see it. And she sees herself.

That is how the world gets rebuilt—one brave kid, one calm grownup at a time.

This is the quiet revolution. The one that saves us. Not with noise but with grit and truth and hope growing inside the next generation when we have the courage to step back and let them climb.

Final Chapter:
See You Out There

You made it to the end. Congratulations. You've now read more pages than most people will read all year, unless you count doomscrolling Twitter You threads about why eggs are suddenly racist.

If you're nodding along, good. If you're mad, also good. If you're confused about whether you're allowed to be both, welcome to 2026—we'll get you a pamphlet.

Either way, the book did what it was supposed to do.

I didn't write this so I could smile on morning shows sipping lukewarm coffee while someone named Brayden asks me "what my journey has been like." I didn't write it to get patted on the back by people who think the world is fine if you just breathe deeper, manifest harder, and buy their $47 workbook on emotional resilience (shipping not included).

I wrote it because I see good people every day—working, trying, showing up, not posting about it—walking around like they've been tricked into believing the world has gone completely nuts and it's somehow their fault for noticing.

It isn't your fault.

The rules changed while we were busy raising kids, paying bills, and keeping the lights on. The game got built by people who've never changed a tire, never missed a mortgage payment, and sure as hell never paid the price for their own ideas.

And somewhere along the way, we forgot something important:

There are more of us than them. A lot more.

They just have better Wi-Fi and more time to argue.

So, here's what matters now:

Close the book. Put the phone away. Look up.

Coach a Little League team that still keeps score—yes, with winners and losers, because that's how baseball works and also how life works. Take your kid magnet fishing even if you drag up nothing but rusty junk and one extremely confused catfish. Let your daughter climb the wall and only help if she asks for it. Tell the truth once tomorrow at work, even if it costs you something—like Todd's approval, which you never had anyway.

Shake hands with the guy wearing the shirt you hate. Mean it. He's probably thinking the same thing about your Crocs, and honestly, he's not wrong.

Eat dinner at the table with the screens off. Make your bed. Fix what's broken. Love your people hard. Apologize when you screw up. Tip the waitress. Hold the door. Say "thank you" like you mean it, not like you're checking a box on your daily gratitude app.

Do the small, stubborn, ordinary things that no algorithm can monetize and no policy can outlaw.

That is how this ends—not with a march or a viral post or a flaming hot take that gets 40,000 retweets and changes exactly nothing. It ends with millions of regular people quietly choosing what's real. Choosing grit over theater. Choosing community over mobs. Choosing to raise kids who can take a hit, stand back up, and not immediately tweet about their trauma.

The revolution isn't coming.

It already started.

It looks like a grandfather on an afternoon watching his granddaughter ring the bell at the top of a plastic tower... and knowing in that one bright second that we are going to be okay.

Not because some politician promised it.

Not because we finally agreed on everything.

But because that little girl just learned she's tougher than she thought, and nobody had to pass a law or start a nonprofit to make it happen.

We don't need permission. We don't need a movement. We don't need another task force, focus group, or listening session where nothing gets heard.

We just need to remember who we are.

So, step off the porch and into the real world. Act like the country still makes sense—not because it does, but because if we do, it will.

Common sense didn't die with fireworks and speeches. It slipped quietly out the back door while we were yelling about hashtags. The funeral was empty. Nobody even brought a casserole. The consequences are still here, though, eating everything in the fridge and asking what's for dinner.

We fix them by how we live. Not what we post.

Thank you for reading this book. I hope you enjoyed it, or at least didn't throw it across the room. And while you're out there living your life, keep this one simple rule in your pocket:

Don't be an asshole.

Seriously. That's it.

Don't cut people off in traffic and then act like they're the problem. Don't scream at teenagers making minimum wage because your latte came out wrong. Don't lecture strangers on the internet about things you Googled five minutes ago. Don't lie when the truth would work just fine. Don't film everything hoping it goes viral. Don't treat people like NPCs in your personal video game.

Just... don't be an asshole.

If we all did that—if we all committed to being 10% less terrible to each other—this book wouldn't need to exist.

Hell, half of Twitter wouldn't need to exist.

(Actually, that's still true either way.)

So that's it. That's the book. No fancy ending. No dramatic mic drop. No call to "join the movement" or "follow me on social media for more life-changing wisdom."

Just this:

Go outside. Talk to your neighbor. Let the kid climb. Fix the thing. Love your people. Tell the truth. Do the work.

The world doesn't need another hero.

It needs a few million regular people who remember that common sense, decency, and effort are not old-fashioned ideas that expired sometime between MySpace and TikTok.

They're how we've always survived.

And they're how we'll survive this, too.

See you out there.

Again, thank you for reading this,

Roger Monarch Jr.

P.S. — If you bought this book, thank you. If you borrowed it, buy your own damn copy. If you

pirated it as a PDF, well... at least you read it. Go do something decent to balance the karma.

www.ingramcontent.com/pod-product-compliance
Lightning Source LLC
Chambersburg PA
CBHW051418090426
42737CB00014B/2720